I0185346

THE FIVE GIANTS

THE FIVE GIANTS

And other Tales

BY

REV. RICHARD NEWTON, D.D.

Author of " The King's Highway," " The Safe Compass,"
" Bible Jewels," &c.

———◦———

SOLID GROUND CHRISTIAN BOOKS
PORT ST LUCIE, FLORIDA USA

SOLID GROUND CHRISTIAN BOOKS
1682 SW PANCOAST STREET
PORT ST LUCIE, FL 34987
205-587-4480
www.solid-ground-books.com
mike.sgcb@gmail.com

THE FIVE GIANTS AND HOW TO FIGHT THEM

By Richard Newton (1813-1887)

First Solid Ground Edition April 2018

Taken from 19th century edition by Gall and Inglis,
Edinburgh and Paternoster Square, London

Cover Design by Borgo Design, Tuscaloosa, Alabama

ISBN: 978-159925-3794

TABLE OF CONTENTS

CHAPTER ONE – THE GIANTS   1

CHAPTER TWO – THE FIRST GIANT: *Heathenism*   5

CHAPTER THREE – THE SECOND GIANT: *Selfishness*   11

CHAPTER FOUR – THE THIRD GIANT: *Covetousness*   16

CHAPTER FIVE – THE FOURTH GIANT: *Ill-Temper*   22

CHAPTER SIX – THE FIFTH GIANT: *Intemperance*   27

CHAPTER SEVEN – THE FIRST REASON FOR FIGHTING   38

CHAPTER EIGHT – THE SECOND REASON FOR FIGHTING   41

CHAPTER NINE – THE THIRD REASON FOR FIGHTING   51

CHAPTER TEN – THE FOURTH REASON FOR FIGHTING   58

CHAPTER ELEVEN – THE GOOD SOLDIERS   76

CHAPTER TWELVE – THE CONQUERORS JEWEL   96

CHAPTER THIRTEEN – THE WONDERFUL EYES   118

CHAPTER FOURTEEN – ACKNOWLEDGING GOD   139

CHAPTER FIFTEEN – THE CURE FOR CARE   166

THE FIVE GIANTS

And How To Fight Them.

CHAPTER I.

THE GIANTS.

"So David prevailed over the Philistine with a sling and with a stone, and smote the Philistine, and slew him."—(1 *Sam.* xvii. 50.) The Philistine spoken of here was the giant Goliath. Now let us put the word Giant instead of the Philistine, and then the text will read in this way:—" So David prevailed over the giant with a sling and a stone, and smote the giant and slew him." All young people like to hear and read stories about giants. I suppose there is hardly a person in this country who knows how to read but who has read the famous history of "Jack the Giant Killer." I remember, when a very little boy, reading it, and thinking what a wonderful history it was. I need not tell you, however, that that history has not a word of truth in it. No such person as the celebrated "Jack" ever lived. And the giants he is said to have killed so nimbly never lived either.

But the verse we have taken for our text to-day tells us about David the Giant Killer. He was a real person. He actually lived about 3000 years ago. And the giant whom he killed was a real live giant. He was a pretty big fellow, too, though not so enormously large as some of the story books would lead us to think. Such huge monsters as they represent never existed anywhere, except in the thoughts of those who write books of fables and stories that are not true. Goliath, the giant whom David killed, was six cubits and a span in height.

There are different opinions about the size of the Jewish measure called a cubit. One of these opinions is that it was twenty-one inches and about two-thirds of an inch. At this rate, six cubits would be about eleven feet four inches. A span is six inches. This added to the other would give us eleven feet ten inches as Goliath's height. Now take two men, each of whom is five feet eleven inches high; let one of them stand upon the head of the other, making, as it were, one man; and suppose him to be stout and strong in proportion to his height, and then you would have a man of about Goliath's size. The coat of mail that he wore weighed about 150 pounds. His armour altogether weighed about 272. That is nearly as much as five fifty-six pound weights. The armour of an ordinary soldier in those times weighed about sixty pounds. How frightful it must have been to see this vast creature, with all his armour on, and his huge spear in his hand, stalk forth before all the army of the Israelites, and dare any one of them to come out and fight with him! We do not wonder that all the soldiers fled away at his approach, and that no one was willing to go and fight him. And we admire very much the courage of David, and his confidence in God, that he, a mere shepherd's boy, was willing, with nothing in his hand but a sling and a stone, to go and do battle with this great giant. You know how angry the giant was when he saw this beardless boy come against him; and what dreadful things he threatened to do to David; and how David ran and took a stone, and slung it; and how it went whizzing along, till it hit him in the forehead, and he fell senseless to the ground.

Some people pretend to think that it was hardly possible for David to throw a stone with sufficient force to sink into the giant's head. One of this class, a foolish young man, who pretended not to believe the Bible, was once riding in a stage-coach, which was full of passengers. He was trying to ridicule some of the Bible stories. Among others he spoke of this one about David and the giant. He said he thought the giant's head must have been too hard for a boy like David to send a stone into it; and turning to an old Quaker gentleman, who sat in the corner of the coach, he asked, "What do you think about it, sir?"

"Friend," said the old gentleman, in a dry, quiet way, "I'll tell thee what I think; if the giant's head was as soft as thine, it must have been very easy for the stone to get in."

But David DID kill the giant. Yes, and we read about several of the giant's brothers who were killed in David's time. The whole family of them was destroyed. But the giants are not all dead yet. THERE ARE giants in the earth in these days. And God expects us all to engage in the work of trying to fight them. When I speak of giants, now, I do not mean physical giants, but moral giants. I do not mean men with huge bodies, four or five times larger than common sized men; but I mean great sins of different kinds, which may well be called giants.

I want now to speak about five giants that we should all unite in trying to fight against. One of these is a good way off from us; but the rest are very near us. Listen to me, while I tell you who these giants are, and the way in which we must try to fight them.

CHAPTER II.

THE first giant I am to speak of is the GIANT HEATHENISM.

This giant doesn't live here. He is found in countries where the Gospel is not known. His castles may be seen in Africa, and in India, in China, and in the islands of the sea. He is a huge giant. He has a great many heads, more indeed than I can pretend to count. In every country where idols are worshipped one of the heads of this giant may be found. One of these heads is called Juggernaut; another is called Brahma; another Buddha, and many such like names. This giant is very strong and very cruel. We read, in that interesting book called "Pilgrim's Progress," about a giant whose name was Despair, and who lived in a castle called "Doubting Castle." He used to seize the pilgrims to the heavenly city as they ventured on his grounds. When he had caught them, he used to thrust them into a dark, dismal dungeon, and beat them with his great

5

club; and treat them so badly that many of them were driven to kill themselves. He was a very strong giant, and very cruel. And Heathenism the giant of whom I am speaking, is just like him in these respects.

HE IS VERY STRONG. He is so strong that he keeps six hundred millions of people in his dungeons all the time. They are bound hand and foot. They cannot possibly get out till the friends of Jesus attack the giant, and make him let go of them.

And he is VERY CRUEL, as well as very strong. The things that are done in some of the dungeons where he dwells show how cruel he is. Look at India. There is Juggernaut, one of the heads of this giant. This idol is kept on a great heavy car. At certain seasons of the year, when they have a festival, this car is dragged out. Hundreds of people take hold of the rope and pull it along; and while it rolls on, great numbers of men and women will throw themselves down before the car, and be crushed to death under its wheels as they roll over them. For miles around the temple you may see the bones of the poor creatures who have been crushed in this way.

In other parts of his dungeon this giant makes his poor wretched prisoners put iron hooks through the flesh on the back of their bodies—and then swing themselves round, with the whole weight of their bodies resting on these hooks.

In other parts, he makes his poor prisoners kill a great many of their little innocent children as soon as they are born. Sometimes their parents will dig a hole in the ground and bury their baby alive in it. Sometimes they will throw them into the river, to be drowned or devoured by alligators. In some places along the river Ganges, there are crocodiles that live almost altogether on the dear little babies that are thrown in by their cruel mothers, to be devoured alive by those horrible monsters.

In the South Sea Islands, three out of four of all the children born used to be killed.

In one tribe of people in India, that numbered 12,000 men, there were only thirty women. All the rest had been killed when they were young.

In the city of Pekin many infants are thrown out into the streets every night. Sometimes they are killed at once by the fall. Sometimes they are only half killed, and linger, moaning in agony, till the morning. Then the police go round and pick them up, and throw them, all together, into a hole, and bury them.

In Africa, the children are sometimes burnt alive.

In India, they are sometimes exposed in the woods till they either starve to death, or are devoured by the jackals and vultures. In the South Sea Islands they used sometimes to strangle their babies; while at other times they would break all their joints, first their fingers and toes, then their ankles and wrists, and then their elbows and knees.

Surely they are horrible dungeons in which such dreadful things are done.

And the giant Heathenism, who makes his prisoners do such things must be indeed a cruel giant.

Well, what are we to do to this giant? Why, we must FIGHT him, as David did Goliath. We do not expect to kill him outright. He will never be killed till Jesus comes again. He Himself will kill the giant Heathenism. But we can cut off some of the giant's heads, and set some of his prisoners free. We are bound in duty to fight against this giant. But how are we to do this? Just as David did. He fought against Goliath with a sling and a stone. He picked the stones out of the brook, and hurled them at the giant. And this is what we must do. The Bible is the brook to which we must go. The truth which it contains are the stones that we must use. When these truths are hurled against the head of this giant, they will sink into it just as David's pebble did into Goliath's head—and he will fall.

A Chinese idolator had become a Christian. He stood among his countrymen one day distributing some tracts. They were taken into the interior of China and read. The reading of them led the people of many towns and villages to give up the worship of idols. This destroyed one of the heads of the giant. In the Sandwich Islands another of his heads has been destroyed;—and another in the islands of New Zealand;—and another in the Feejee Islands. And Sunday-school children are trying to help in this work, when they assist in making contributions to the missionary cause. We are helping to throw the stones of truth at the heads of the giant Heathenism. When the missionaries preach of Jesus to the heathen, they are slinging stones at the giant's head. God directs the stones which they throw, and makes them effectual to wound and disable the giant. David never could have killed Goliath if left to himself. But God helped him, and then the stone did its work. And so God will help us; so He will help all who fight against the great cruel giant— Heathenism. Then let us go on, like brave giant-killers, and fight against this giant. We are sure to succeed—for God has promised that the giant shall be killed at last.

The first giant is HEATHENISM: and we are to fight against him by throwing stones of truth at him.

But now let us go on to speak of some other giants. The one I have just spoken of lives a great way on from us. The others we are to fight against live near us. They may be found in our own country;—in our own city;—in our own homes;—yes, and even in our own HEARTS.

CHAPTER III.

THE SECOND GIANT.

THE second giant I would speak of is the GIANT SELFISHNESS.

Now, remember, I am not speaking of physical giants, but moral giants ;—not of giants made of flesh and blood, but of giants made of thoughts and feelings. This giant Selfishness is an intensely ugly looking creature. If he could be caught, in a bodily shape, and carried to some photographer's office to have his likeness taken, I am sure that, when you came to look at his picture, you would think it about the ugliest you had ever seen.

How many eyes have you? Two. How many ears? Two. How many hands? Two. And how many feet? Two. Yes, God has given us each two eyes, two ears, two hands, and two feet, as if it were to remind us that we are to see, and hear, and work, and walk, for others, as well as for ourselves. But how many mouths have you? One. Yes, for we have to eat for ourselves only, and not for others. But the giant Selfishness never sees, or hears, or does anything for any one but himself. If we had a correct likeness of him, we should see a huge one-eyed, one-eared, one-armed monster, with his other eye, and ear, and arm shrivelled, and dried up like a mummy's, for want of use. The business of this giant is to take people prisoners, and drag them to his castle. If they stay, there long, they begin to grow just like him, ugly one-sided looking creatures. I do not mean to say, that this change takes place in their bodies, but it does in their souls. They learn to love none but themselves. They think and care for none but themselves. This giant is trying all the time to bind his chains on people, and make them his prisoners. He likes especially to do this while they are young.

But if he does not appear in a bodily form, how may we know when he is trying to fasten his chains on us and make us his prisoners?

Let me tell you. If you find that you are getting to think more of YOURSELF than of others, then be sure the giant is after you. If you see a boy, or girl, enter a room, and go and take the best seat in it when older persons are present; if you see them pick out for themselves the largest piece of cake, or the biggest and nicest apple, when these are handed round, you may be sure the giant Selfishness is at work on them. He is fastening his chains upon them; and if they don't take care, he will soon have them as his prisoners.

Now, we must ALL FIGHT this giant. But HOW are we to do this? Not by standing off at a distance and throwing stones at him, as we are to do with the giant HEATHENISM. This will not do here. No, THIS must be a close, hand-to-hand fight. We must grapple him, and wrestle with him. WE MUST FIGHT THIS GIANT BY SELF-DENIAL.

Let me show you what I mean by this. There were two little boys, named James and William. One day, as they were just starting for school, their father gave them each a three-cent piece to spend for themselves. The little fellows were very much pleased with this, and went off, as merry as crickets.

"What are you going to buy, William?" said James, after they had walked a little way.

"I don't know," William replied, "I have not thought yet. What are you going to buy?"

"Why, I tell you what I believe I'll do. You know mother is sick. Now, I think I'll buy her a nice orange. I think it will taste good to her."

"You may do so if you please, James," said William; but I'm going to buy something for

MYSELF. Father gave me the money to spend for myself, and I mean to do it. If mother wants an orange she can send for it. She's got money, and Hannah gets every thing she wants."

"I know that," said James, "but then it would make me feel so happy to see her eating an orange that I had bought for her with my own money. She is always doing something for us, or getting us some nice thing, and I want to let her see that I don't forget it."

"Do as you please," said William, "but I go in for the candy."

Presently they came to the confectioner's shop. William invested his three cents in cream-candy, but James bought a nice orange. When they went home at noon, he went into his mother's chamber, and said: "See, Ma', what a nice orange I have brought you!"

"It is, indeed, very nice, my son, and it will taste very good to me. I have been wanting an orange all the morning. Where did you get it ?"

"Pa' gave me three cents this morning, and I bought it with them."

"You are very good, my dear boy, to think of your sick mother. And you wouldn't spend your money for cakes, or candy, but denied yourself, that you might get an orange for me. Mother loves you for this exercise of self-denial." And then she threw her arms around his neck, and kissed him.

Now, here you see how the giant Selfishness made an attack on these two boys. James fought him off bravely by the EXERCISE OF SELF-DENIAL. William refused to exercise self-denial, and so the giant got a hitch of his chain around him. We shall find this giant making attacks upon us all the time. We can only fight him off by SELF-DENIAL.

CHAPTER IV.

THE THIRD GIANT.

THE third giant I want to speak about is the
GIANT COVETOUSNESS.

This giant is very large in size, and very strong
in limb; but he has the tiniest little bit of a heart
you ever saw. It isn't bigger than a Bantam
chicken's heart. You might put it in a nutshell.
The only wonder is how so huge a frame can be
supported by so little a heart. But this is not
all, for little as his heart is, it is as hard as a
stone. We sometimes hear of people dying with
what is called the OSSIFICATION of the heart. Ossification means turning to bone. When a man's
heart gets hard, or turns to bone, he dies. According to this rule the giant Covetousness ought
to have been dead long ago. It's a perfect wonder
how he manages to live, with his little heart all
turned to stone. But he DOES live; yes, and not
only lives, but is hearty and strong. He is very
active. His castle is of great size, and he always
has it crowded with prisoners. Those whom he

once fairly gets into his chains, find it very hard
to break loose. Yet this is very strange, for he
is a most disagreeable creature. He drives the
poor away from his door. If a shivering beggar
comes by, he buttons up his pocket, lest by any
means a penny should happen to get out. He can
hear about poor widows and orphans starving
with hunger, and perishing with cold, but never
sheds a tear, or heaves a sigh, or gives the least
trifle for their relief. When he knows of worthy
people being in need, he "shutteth up his com-
passion from them." His heart is hard as a rock,
and cold as an iceberg. He loves money better
than anything else in the world. He gets all he
can, and keeps all he gets. He is ashamed of his
name, and wont answer to it. He pretends that
his right name is—FRUGALITY. But this is a great
story. Frugality is a very different person. He
is a good, true, honest fellow. I know he is a
sort of SECOND COUSIN of the giants, and some
people think he looks very much like him, but
I don't think he does at all. At any rate this is
NOT the giant's name. His own, real, proper name
is COVETOUSNESS; and his puny, little, stony heart
PROVES it.

Well, his prisoners all become wonderfully like
him. Their hearts shrivel up till they are almost

as little and as hard as his. But how may we know when he is trying to make people his prisoners? Very easily. When you see people learning to love their money more than they used to do;—when they always tie their purse-strings very tight, and are very slow to untie them;—when you hear them all the time grumbling about there being so many collections taken up,—and so many calls for money;—when you find them unwilling to give;—when you see them wince and wriggle under parting with a little money, as though you were drawing one of their eye-teeth out of their heads, then you may know that the giant Covetousness has got a hold upon these people.

My dear children, I want you all to fight bravely against this giant. If you ask, How are you to fight him, I answer, By LEARNING TO GIVE. He hates giving above all things. It hurts his feelings dreadfully. Once get into the habit of giving, and he never can fasten his chains upon you.

"Mother," asked a little boy who was trying to make a good beginning of the new year, "How much of my spending money do you think I ought to give to God?"

"I don't know," said his mother—"How much have you?" He opened his wallet, and out dropped on the table a gold dollar his grandmother had given him for a Christmas present, a five-cent piece, and a three-cent piece.

"There's my gold dollar,—I'll halve that," said he; "five cents and three cents are eight cents, and half of that is four. But, no. I'll GIVE THE LARGEST HALF TO GOD. I'll give Him half the dollar and the five cents."

I don't believe the giant Covetousness will ever get a single link of his chain fastened on the limbs of that noble-hearted boy.

But I want to tell you about a great battle once fought, between this giant and a Deacon in a church of New England. We may call the Deacon's name Holdfast. The story is a true one, though this was not the man's real name. Before Deacon Holdfast became a Christian, he had been a prisoner of the giant's for years. The chains had been so riveted upon his limbs that he found it very hard to get rid of them. Many a sharp conflict they had together. Sometimes the Deacon would get the victory, but more frequently the giant. Still the Deacon wouldn't give up. He was determined not to wear the giant's chain. And after the fight that I'm going to tell you about, he got such an advantage over the giant that he never troubled him much again. It happened in this way.

In the same church to which the Deacon belonged, there was a worthy, honest, good man who was very poor. This poor man had the misfortune to lose his cow. She died. The poor man was in great distress. The cow was his chief dependence for the support of his family. He went and told the Deacon about his trouble. In order to aid him in getting another cow, the good Deacon drew up a subscription-paper, and put his own name down at the head of it for five dollars, which he paid over. This made the giant Covetousness very angry. He took on dreadfully. He began to rave and storm, and tried to frighten the Deacon.

"What's the use of all this waste?" he cried. "Charity begins at home. The more you give the more you may give. Why can't you let people take care of themselves? What right have you to take the bread out of the mouths of your own children and give it to strangers? Go on at this rate, and the poor-house, wretchedness, poverty, and rags are what you will come to."

This made the Deacon angry. His spirit was roused. He went to the poor man to whom he had given the subscription, and told him he must give him back the five dollars. The poor fellow's heart sunk within him. He thought he should never get his cow again. But he handed over the money. The Deacon stood a moment as if hesitating what to do. At last he said to the poor man:—" My brother, some people are very much troubled with their old women, but I am troubled with my OLD MAN. He has been scolding me dreadfully for giving you so much money; but now I mean to fix him." And then turning round as if addressing the giant, he said:—" Old fellow, I want you to understand that I mean to give away just as much money as I think right." And then opening his wallet and taking out a ten dollar bill, he added,—" I shall now give this good brother ten dollars instead of five, and if you say another word I'll give him TWENTY instead of ten."

This was a dreadful blow to the giant. It laid him sprawling on the ground. It took him, as the Bible says, "under the fifth rib." It knocked the breath clean out of him. He hadn't a word to say.

LEARNING TO GIVE is the way in which to fight the giant Covetousness.

CHAPTER V.

THE FOURTH GIANT.

THE fourth giant of which I will speak is the GIANT ILL-TEMPER.

This giant is not so large or strong as the others, but he is quite as ugly. He is found in more places than the last. He has more to do with young people than either of the others, though he does attack old people too, sometimes. He is always in a pet. From constant pouting his lips have grown horribly thick and ugly-looking. He is frowning all the time, till his forehead is as full of wrinkles and as rough as the bark of an old oak tree. Sometimes his eyes are red with weeping, and at other times they are all in a flame with anger. Sometimes his voice bellows like thunder, and then again it will resemble the low hoarse growl of a surly dog.

He may generally be found hanging round the nursery, the dining, or sitting-room, ready to pounce upon the children and make them prisoners. And when he gets hold of them he makes them so ugly and disagreeable that no one cares to have anything to do with them.

Now let me give you some signs by which you may know when this giant is getting hold of a boy or girl. He generally waits and watches till he hears them asked to do something which he knows they don't like. Then he is ready in a moment to begin his attack. He makes the eye begin to frown. He puckers up the mouth; he makes the lips pout and swell out to twice their usual size. The fingers begin to wriggle about like a set of worms; or sometimes one of the fingers goes into the corner of the mouth. The shoulders are seen to twist about, first one way, and then another. If the boy has a book in his hand down it drops on the floor, or else it is flung across the room. If he is walking, he stamps with his foot, as if he were trying to get a tight shoe on. If he is sitting, his feet begin to swing backwards and forwards, and make a great noise by striking against the chair. Sometimes he seems to become deaf and dumb. He hears nothing, and says nothing. At other times he speaks, but it is just like a dog when snarling over a bone.

Whenever you see these signs you may know that this ugly giant is about, and is busy making prisoners. And if you don't fight bravely against him he will fasten his chains on you, and then you will be spoiled.

BUT HOW ARE WE TO FIGHT AGAINST THIS GIANT? I answer:—BY TRYING TO BE LIKE JESUS.

We always think of Him as—the "gentle Jesus meek and mild." Do you suppose that this giant ever got a single link of his chain on Jesus? No. Do you suppose Jesus ever spoke a cross word to any one? No. Do you suppose He ever did an unkind act to any one? No. We have no particular history of the childhood of Jesus. But we know how He acted when He was a man; and we know that He was always the same. If we try to be like Jesus the giant Ill-temper will never get hold of us. When you are tempted to speak cross words, or to do unkind things, ask yourself the question, What would Jesus do or say if He were in my situation? In this way you will always be able to fight off this giant.

I was reading lately about two little sisters who always lived happily together. The giant Ill-temper never could catch them. They had the same books and the same playthings, yet they never quarrelled. No cross words, no pouts, no slaps, no running away in a pet, ever took place with them. Whether they were sitting on the green before the door, or playing with their old dog Congo, or dressing their dolls, or helping their mother, they were always the same sweet-tempered little girls.

"You never seem to quarrel," said a lady visiting at their house one day. "How is it that you are always so happy together?"

They looked up, and the eldest answered, "I 'spose it's 'cause ADDIE LETS ME, AND I LET ADDIE."

Ah! yes, it's just THIS LETTING that keeps the giant off. What a beautiful picture that is of those sweet-tempered sisters! But see what a different one this is:

A mother hears a noise under the window. She looks out.

"Gerty, what's the matter?"

"Mary won't let me have her ball," cries Gerty.

"Well, Gerty wouldn't let me have her pencil in school," cries Mary, "and I don't mean she shall have my ball."

"Fie, fie, is that the way for sisters to act towards each other?" says the mother.

"She'll only lose my pencil," mutters Gerty, "and she sha'n't have it."

"And she'll only lose my ball," replies Mary "and I won't let her have it."

Ah! the giant had got fast hold of these two girls. They didn't know how to fight him. They were not trying to be like Jesus.

CHAPTER VI.

THE FIFTH GIANT.

THE last giant I wish to speak about is the GIANT INTEMPERANCE.

When a person is making a speech, and giving reasons to persuade those who hear him to do anything, he generally keeps the strongest reason for the last. And so I have put the giant Intemperance last, and shall say more about him than any of the others, because he is the most important. He is the worst giant of the whole lot, as I think you will be ready to own after you have heard a little about him.

He is a very ugly looking fellow. When he is in a good humour, and feels jolly, he puts on a silly face, and looks very foolish. But when he gets into a passion he is awful looking, and it makes one shudder to see him. He never was very handsome even when he was quite young; but as he has grown older and more wicked, evil passions have shown themselves more and more on his countenance, and sin has stamped its

27

dreadful mark upon his features so fearfully, that
he is now a very monster of ugliness. And he is
so filthy, too, that his whole appearance is dis-
gusting.   Generally he is clothed in rags.   Often
he is seen covered with dirt, gathered from the
gutter where he has been lying.   His face is
frequently all bruised and swollen from the fights
in which he has been engaging.   Sometimes he
goes unwashed and unshaved for days together;
and then, with a rough, shaggy beard, and with
an old crumpled hat on his head, he may be
seen reeling and staggering about the streets, a
perfect nuisance to the neighbourhood.

He is very wicked, too.   He breaks every com-
mandment of God's law.   He is the author of
nearly every crime that is committed.   It is he
who sets on men and women to sin.   He fills our
almshouses, our prisons, and penitentiaries.   If it
were not for him we might dismiss most of our
police, do without half our courts, close our station-
houses, tear down our prisons, and burn our galleys.
Sin follows him like a shadow wherever he goes.
Quarrelling, swearing, fighting, robbing, murdering,
and all kinds of wickedness abound where this
giant dwells.

Of all the giants in this country he is the
largest, the most powerful, and in every way the

most dangerous. He is stronger here than almost anywhere else. There was a time when he might easily have been driven out of the land. But now he has built so many castles and gloomy dungeons; he has so many thousands of men in his service, and so much money to use in his defence, that he bids defiance to his enemies. More sermons and speeches have been delivered against him, more books written, more societies formed, and more efforts made in every way against him, than all the rest put together.

And though he is thousands of years old, and has been through hundreds of battles, he does not seem to grow weak or stiff with age like giant Paganism, that Bunyan tells of in the "Pilgrim's Progress." But every year he seems to get stronger and more active. And oh! what a sad sight it is to look into his dungeons! Hundreds and thousands of prisoners in our land are bound fast in his chains. He has more of them than any other giant here. And they are not from any one class only. The rich and the poor, the high and the low, are among them. Labouring men, mechanics, merchants, lawyers, doctors, ministers; men and women, and even children too, are dragged into his dungeons. The most accomplished, the most talented, the most beautiful, the most amiable, fall under his power. Thirty thousand captives are taken from his dungeons in our own country every year, and buried in a drunkard's grave. How dreadful this is to think of!

We read in history that, a good many years ago, when Greece was one of the first nations of the world, there was a great monster who troubled a part of that land very much. He made them send him every year seven boys and seven girls. These he used to eat. And every year when the time came for sending these poor children, what a scene of sorrow there was! How the parents cried, and how the friends and relatives cried! And how those who were going to be slaughtered cried, as they went on board the great ship with black sails that carried the victims to the monster. Those people thought it was a terrible thing to have that dreadful plague devour FOURTEEN of their children every year. But what was that Grecian monster in comparison with this awful giant Intemperance? He takes THIRTY THOUSAND men, and women, and children every year, and devours them.

Of course, he must be very busy making prisoners to be able to take so many. He sets a great many traps and snares to catch people.

The taverns, grog-shops, lager-beer houses, and drinking saloons, along our streets, are all TRAPS he has set. There he sits watching to catch any passer-by, just as you often see a spider quietly waiting in its web to entangle some poor fly. Into these traps people are enticed. They are tempted to drink. They learn to love drinking. And when this habit is formed they become his prisoners. But these are not his only snares. He is very cunning, and often catches people where they have no idea there is any danger.

Sometimes he puts little traps inside of tempting looking sugar-plums to catch boys and girls. He drops a little wine, or cordial, or brandy, into these sugar-plums, and then spreads them out in the store windows. These are bought and eaten. The taste for liquor is formed, and so by degrees the giant fastens his chain upon the buyers, till they, too, become his prisoners.

Sometimes he spreads a snare in the social evening party. A pleasant company is assembled. Refreshments are handed round. Wine is poured out. A young man is asked to take some, but declines. He is pressed to drink to the health of a friend. He hesitates, not wishing to hurt his friend's feelings, but thinks he can't refuse without doing so. The sparkling glass is taken. Then

another, and another, till at last he is intoxicated.
The giant has fastened the first link of his cruel
chain upon him. The taste for drink is formed
now. He wants more and more. By and bye he
can't do without it. The giant has bound him
hand and foot, and he is dragged helplessly down
to ruin.

These are some of his ways of catching people.
He does not pounce upon them and drag them off
at once, but he captures them by degrees. Do you
know how a boa-constrictor seizes a sheep or a
cow ? When he sees one coming he darts suddenly
forth, throws a part of his huge body around the
animal, then another, and another, till he has
bound it so tight that it cannot move. It is
unable to resist then, and the serpent crushes it
to death in his powerful folds. Well, just so
this giant fights. He does not bind his prisoners
fast at once, but winds himself gradually about
them. Every time they drink liquor he throws a
fold around them. Tighter and tighter he grasps
them, until he has them completely in his power.
When you see a person beginning to drink intoxicating liquor of any kind, be sure the giant
is after him. You may always know when he is
coming, and I will tell you how. Did you ever
see a shark ? You know what horrible creatures

they are, and how much the sailors dread them.
They will bite off a man's leg, or even swallow
him whole, and make nothing of it. Well, you
can always tell when a shark is about. He sends
a little fish ahead of him called the pilot-fish.
If you see one of these about the vessel, then
look out for a shark. He is certainly near, and
you will soon see him. Now, the giant Intemperance always sends a sort of pilot-fish ahead of
him. He never comes before it, but is pretty
sure to come after it. Wherever you see it look
out for the giant. Do you know what it is? It
is A BOTTLE OR DECANTER. When you see one of
these in use you may be sure the giant is not
far off.

When a person gets into his power, everything
begins to go wrong with him. His business is
neglected. His money is squandered. He becomes
unkind to his wife and children, or undutiful to
his parents. He spends for drink that which
should go to support his family. He becomes
cruel and hard-hearted, passionate and fierce. His
evil tempers are roused. They conquer his better
feelings. He turns from the path of virtue and
enters that of vice. That is a down-hill path, and
the giant pushes him on faster and faster. He
loses all sense of shame, and hesitates not at any

sin. There is nothing so mean, so base, so wicked, that the prisoner of this giant will not do. His prospects for the future are ruined the moment he is securely bound. Yes, RUINED: ruined for time and for eternity. Misery, poverty, disgrace and want are the portion the giant gives him while he lives; and when he dies he finds the truth of the Bible statement, that "drunkards shall NOT inherit the kingdom of God."

This giant Intemperance is the one we are now to speak about. Is he not a horrible fellow? And should we not all engage in fighting him?

Now, there are two things for us to consider:— HOW WE ARE TO FIGHT HIM; and WHY WE SHOULD FIGHT HIM. The way in which, and the reason why, we ought to fight him.

By fighting this giant Intemperance I don't mean going into his dungeons and trying to get his prisoners out. This we ought to do with all our hearts whenever we can. But the kind of fighting I am going now to talk about is what soldiers would call DEFENSIVE WARFARE,—that is, how to keep him off from OURSELVES, so that he shall not make us his prisoners.

We are to do this BY DRINKING COLD WATER. Of course, I do not mean to put cold water in opposition to milk, or tea, or coffee. If we only

keep to such drinks as these, the giant's hands
will never be laid on us. But I mean cold water
in opposition to cider, beer, wine, brandy, gin, and
the like, as our habitual drink.

Some people say that it does no harm to drink
A LITTLE. Let us see whether this is so or not.

Suppose you were on the top of a high mountain, and wanted to amuse yourself by rolling a
large stone down its side. Some one standing by
objects to this sport, telling you that it may,
perhaps, fall on the head of a traveller climbing
up the mountain, and crush him to death ; or
break through the roof of some cottage far down
in the valley.

"Oh! no," you reply, "I only intend to roll it
a LITTLE WAY. I don't mean to let it go far
enough to do any mischief." But if you bring it
to the edge, and push it over, can you stop it
when you please ? Of course not. The easiest, the
safest, the ONLY way to prevent any danger
would be NOT TO SET IT IN MOTION AT ALL.

Just so it is with drinking. There is no danger
while we keep to cold water, and let all kinds of
liquor alone. But if we begin taking a little now
and then we shall soon find it hard to stop;
and if the habit goes on increasing it will, before
long, be almost impossible to give it up. Every

cup we take, like each successive roll of the stone, only makes the next more easy.

In the story of Sinbad the sailor we read that, in one of his voyages, he landed on a pleasant island. While walking about there he met a little old man, who asked him if he would be so kind as to help him a little on his journey. Sinbad stooped down, picked him up, and set him on his shoulders. By and bye he began to be tired, and wanted the old man to get down. But he wouldn't. After a little while he asked him again to get off. But still he refused. Then Sinbad tried to shake him off. But he couldn't. The man clung on as if for life. So poor Sinbad had to journey on and on with this load upon his shoulders.

Now, if you let this giant once get hold of you, you will have as much trouble to get rid of him as Sinbad had with the old man. He will probably cling to you for life, and· be a load too heavy for you to bear. The only way is TO KEEP HIM OFF ALTOGETHER.

The great Dr. Johnson used to say that it was easy not to drink at all, but hard to drink a little and not soon take a great deal. There is danger in drinking liquor at all, but there is no danger in not drinking. One thing is certain, if we use only cold water we shall never be made prisoners by this giant. He has no power at all over those who keep to cold water, and none of his attempts can succeed against them.

In Fairy tales we sometimes read about the CHARMS or TALISMANS, which the persons there described are said to wear. These are supposed to have the power of protecting those who use them from all their enemies. No one, it was thought, could harm them while they had these about them. Well, COLD WATER is the talisman for us if we do not want to become prisoners of this giant. He never can conquer us while we make this our drink.

CHAPTER VII.

THE FIRST REASON FOR FIGHTING.

Now, the next thing we were to consider was WHY we should fight against this giant. There are FOUR reasons for doing so in the way spoken of, that is, by the use of cold water.

We should fight against the giant in this way, because COLD WATER IS THE DRINK THAT GOD HAS MADE FOR US.

We have springs and fountains of water all over the world. They are found in every land. Wherever we find people living, there we find water for them to drink. But we never find anything else than water in these springs. Springs differ very much, both in taste and quality. The water from one spring will have sulphur in it; another will have iron in it; another will have magnesia in it; another will have some kind of salt in it; but there never was a spring found in all the world that had alcohol in it. Alcohol, you know, is the part of wine or liquor that intoxicates or makes people drunk. But alcohol is never found in the water that God has made, as it comes gushing up, pure and sparkling, from the earth. Nobody ever heard of a natural spring that yielded lager beer, or ale, or porter, or wine, or gin, or brandy. But if it had been good for us to have such drinks as these, God would have made them. He could have made springs that would yield different kinds of liquor just as easily as He made the trees to bear different kinds of fruit. If it had been necessary for us there would have been in every neighbourhood one or two beer, or ale, or brandy fountains. But you may travel round the globe, from East to West, from North to South; you may visit every country, and examine every stream, and spring, and well, and you will not find anywhere a single beer, or wine, or brandy spring.

When God made Adam and Eve, you know He put them in the beautiful garden of Eden. In that garden, we are told, "the Lord God made to grow every tree that was pleasant to the sight and good for food. And a river went out of Eden to water the garden; and it was parted and came into four heads." This is what the Bible tells us about that garden. We know it must have been very beautiful. Everything that God makes is beautiful. When He makes a

rainbow, how beautiful it is! When He makes
a butterfly, how beautiful it is! When He makes
a flower, a tree, a star, a sun, they are all
beautiful. And when God undertook to make a
garden, oh! how VERY beautiful it must have been!
What gently swelling hills!—what level plains!—
what shady groves!—what velvet lawns!—what
green, mossy banks!—what graceful trees!—what
fragrant flowers!—what springs and fountains of
cool, crystal water were there! Everything that
was pleasant to the eye and to the ear, to the
taste and to the smell was there; but do you
suppose that in any part of the garden of Eden
there was a wine or brandy fountain? No;
nothing of the kind was found there. Well,
then, if cold water was the drink which God gave
Adam in Eden; if cold water is the drink which
God has made for us, and if it is the ONLY DRINK
He has made for us, doesn't it follow very naturally
that cold water is the best drink for us, and the
one that we should use in preference to all others?
And doesn't it follow, too, that we should have
nothing to do with the giant Intemperance, but should
resist him with all our might?

The first reason, then, why we should fight against
the giant Intemperance is because COLD WATER IS
THE DRINK GOD HAS MADE FOR US.

CHAPTER VIII.

THE SECOND REASON FOR FIGHTING.

WE should fight against this Giant because HE IS AN ENEMY TO HEALTH AND STRENGTH.

He never allows a prisoner of his to possess these blessings. He does not take them away at once, but, little by little, he robs every captive of them. The atmosphere of his dungeons is poisonous.

When one has been a captive of this giant for several years, what a picture of disease he presents! He is only the wreck of a man. His strength of body and of mind is gone; and his drooping head, his bloated face, his bloodshot eyes, his trembling hands, and staggering step, tell plainly what the giant has done for him. And then comes the delirium tremens, that dreadful sickness, caught only in this giant's dungeons, with all its horrors, and hurries the poor man off to the drunkard's grave.

And those whom the giant only catches now and then, and who soon escape again from his clutches, do not get off uninjured. And even

41

those who are never really made prisoners, who only take a little, do themselves harm. Many persons do not believe that this is so. They think a little wine or brandy strengthens them and does them good, and that it is only because some people drink too much, and get intoxicated, that there is any harm done by drinking. But liquors will injure if taken at all, though the more we take the worst it will be for us.

Cold water, however, PROMOTES health and strength. There can be no doubt about this; neither can there be any doubt about the bad effect of liquors.

God is the wisest and most skilful physician in the universe. He knows what is best for the health and strength of people, and He prescribes cold water as the best drink.

Some years ago there was a man who had a severe wound in his side. It healed at last, but left an opening with a flap of skin lying over it, and through this opening persons could see right into his stomach. The physician who attended him tried a great many interesting experiments upon him. When he made his patient drink cold water and live on plain food, he found his stomach in a healthy state. When he made him use beer, or wine, or brandy for several days, he found the inside of his stomach inflamed and sore ; and the man would complain of pain in his stomach, and headache, and say he felt very unwell.

There is an interesting story mentioned in the Bible that illustrates this point. You remember when Daniel and his companions went to Babylon, they were chosen, with a number of others, to go through a course of training to fit them for appearing in the presence of the king. While undergoing this training, they were expected to drink wine, and eat certain articles of food which a pious Jew did not feel at liberty to use. The thought of doing this was a great trial to Daniel and his friends. They could not feel willing to do it. They therefore asked the officer who had charge of them to excuse them from eating the meat and drinking the wine which the others used, and allow them to drink water and eat pulse, that is, such things as rice, beans, &c. The officer was a great friend to Daniel, and he said he would be very glad to accommodate him and his friends in this matter, but he was afraid that if he did so they would grow thin and pale, while the rest would be looking hearty and strong; and then, when the king came to see them, he would be displeased at him, and perhaps order his head to be taken off. Then Daniel asked him to be so kind as to try the experiment for ten days and see how it worked. He did so. Daniel and his friends had rice and such like articles for food, and drank water; while the other young men ate meat and drank wine. At the end of ten days the officer found that Daniel and his companions were stouter and healthier than all the rest.

It is a great mistake to suppose that wine and liquors have the effect of making people strong and hearty. They have just the opposite effect. There is no drink that gives more real strength than cold water.

You know how strong the ox and the horse are, and what hard work they have to do, well, what do they drink? Water, and nothing else. Take the horse, or the ox, after he has been ploughing hard all day, and is worn out with fatigue. Offer him a bucket of beer or wine. Will he drink it? Not a drop. But give him a bucket of water, and how quickly he will drink it up. Water gives the horse his strength, and the ox, and the huge elephant, too.

Look at that giant oak tree. How strong it is! Yet it drinks nothing but water. You know that trees DRINK as well as men and cattle. The tree drinks through its roots and through its leaves. If you break the tender stem of a plant or tree you see a milky sort of liquid ooze out. We call it the sap. The sap is to the tree just what the blood is to our bodies. Their growth and strength depend upon it. But water makes the best sap for the trees, as it makes the best blood for our bodies. Take any plant and let it have nothing but wine, or beer, to moisten its leaves and roots, and it will die. Suppose it should rain wine or brandy for six months what would the effect be? All the plants and trees would die.

One day a temperance man met a poor, miserable sailor who had almost ruined himself with drink. He induced him to sign the pledge for one year. Jack liked the improvement in his health and prospects so much that, when the year was out, he went and renewed the pledge for ninety-nine years. He had just received his wages, which he was carrying in a bag in the inner side-pocket of his jacket. It looked like a great lump or swelling there. On his way home he met the tavern-keeper, at whose house he used to spend his wages in liquor, and thought he would have a little fun with him.

"Well, old fellow," said the tavern-keeper, "how do you do?"

"Pretty well," said the sailor, "only I've got a hard lump here on my side."

"Ah!" said the other, "it's cold water that has made that."

"Do you think so?"

"Yes, I know it. Only give up your miserable cold water slops, and drink some good liquor, and it will soon take the lump away."

"But," said the sailor, "I have just renewed the pledge, and I can't do it."

"Then mind what I say," said the tavern-keeper, "that lump will go on increasing, and very likely before another year you'll have one on the other side too."

"I hope I shall," said the sailor, taking out his bag of silver and shaking it. "Good-bye."

Some years ago, a vessel, loaded with iron, was wrecked on the coast of New Jersey in the winter-time. The hold of the vessel was partially filled with water. It was necessary to get the iron out before the vessel went to pieces. The weather was intensely cold, and to stand in the water and handle the cold iron was very severe work. The men hired to unload the vessel were divided into three sets, who were to relieve each other as often as might be necessary. The first set of men drank pretty freely of brandy before they began, in order, as they said, to keep up their strength. They were worn out in about an hour. The next drank hot coffee, and they stood the work for above two hours. The third set were cold water men, and they were able to continue at the work for about three hours before they were relieved.

A good many years ago, the crew of a Danish ship, numbering sixty persons, had to spend the winter up towards the North Pole in Hudson's Bay. They were supplied with provisions, and had plenty of liquor, of which they drank freely. Before spring FIFTY-EIGHT out of the sixty had died, leaving only TWO men to return home. Not long after, the crew of an English vessel, numbering twenty-two men, had to pass a winter in the same neighbourhood. They had no ardent spirits with them, and only TWO of the company died during the whole winter.

When ships, on board of which much liquor is used, go into warm climates, they are always having sickness and death among the crews; but temperance ships will often make the same voyages and hardly have a single case of sickness or death on board. This shows how health follows cold water drinkers, while it flies from the presence of the giant.

But nothing proves this more certainly than to

notice the different effect which disease has on those who are in the habit of drinking liquor, from what it has on those who drink water.

When a dreadful disease like the cholera, or the yellow fever, breaks out, those who drink liquor are the most likely to take it, and the least likely to get well of it. The constant or habitual use of liquor makes the system ripe, or ready for disease.

An English gentleman, who was in Russia while the cholera was prevailing, says:—"It is a remarkable circumstance, that persons given to drinking were swept away like flies. In one town of twenty thousand inhabitants every drunkard has fallen!—all are dead—not one remains!"

A physician in Poland, says:—"The disease spared all those who led regular temperate lives, and lived in healthy situations; but they who were weakened by drinking were always attacked. Out of every hundred individuals destroyed by cholera, it can be proved that NINETY were accustomed to the free use of ardent spirits."

A physician, who was in Montreal at the time the cholera was there, says, that "after there had been one thousand two hundred cases, it was found out that not a single drunkard who

took it recovered; and that almost all who
DID take it, had been at least moderate drinkers."

There were two hundred and four cases of
cholera in the Park Hospital in New York at
one time. Of these, only SIX were temperate
people. They all got well. Of the rest, one hundred and twenty-two died of the disease.

The cholera prevailed very badly in the city of
Albany in 1832. There were then five thousand
members of the temperance society in that city.
Only TWO of them died of the disease. There
were twenty thousand persons there not members
of the temperance society. Among them there
were three hundred and thirty-four deaths from
cholera. Only think of this. Two deaths out of
five thousand temperate people, and MORE THAN
EIGHTY deaths out of every five thousand of those
who were not temperate.

These facts prove very clearly the point we
are considering. They show that cold water helps
to make a man strong and hearty, and keeps
him free from sickness; while wines and brandies,
and all such drinks, weaken those who use them
at all, and make them more likely to take
disease.

And if those who never take enough to be
made prisoners by this giant, who only venture

on his grounds and walk about his castle, without
ever getting fairly entrapped, are so much injured
by the poison that comes forth from his dungeons; how must it be with those who are bound
captives and kept in those dungeons?

Oh! then, we should fight against the giant
Intemperance, and try to keep clear of him,
BECAUSE HE IS AN ENEMY TO HEALTH AND STRENGTH.

CHAPTER IX.

WE should fight against this Giant BECAUSE HE IS AN ENEMY TO SAFETY AND HONOUR.

The giant Intemperance exposes his prisoners to many dangers. He makes them unfit to take care of themselves. They do not know when they are in danger, and, if they did, they are unable to avoid it. When one of them is walking, you expect every minute to see him tumble and break some of his bones. Look in the paper any morning and you are almost sure to see an account of some poor man who has been run over by a locomotive, or drowned by falling off the wharf at night; and nine times out of ten, if you ask how it happened, you will find that he was a captive of the giant. The only wonder is that all his prisoners are not killed thus.

And, of course, if they are unable to take care of themselves, they are unfit to take any care of others. Yet the lives of hundreds of men and women are often put in peril, and some-

51

times lost, by the influence of this giant on one or two persons.

Who would want to trust themselves at sea with a captain and crew who were crazy? Who would want to travel in a train of cars, if they knew that the engineer and conductor were either crazy all the time, or subject at any time to spells of craziness? But a drunken man is no better than a crazy one. And a person in the habit of drinking is liable at any moment to get drunk, and so to become crazy.

But the use of cold water keeps a man from thus losing his reason, and so enables him to see and avoid dangers. It promotes safety. How many of the steamboat explosions and shipwrecks occurring continually might be prevented, if the persons in charge of them were only cold water men!

Some time ago there was a steamboat plying on one of our western rivers. She was called the Fame. Captain Gordon, her commander, was a temperance man, and allowed no liquor to be kept, or used, by any of the officers or crew. About that time a new safety-valve for steam engines had been invented, which it was thought would tend to prevent explosions. It was called "Evan's Patent Safety-Valve." A good many people were unwilling to travel in any steamboat unless it had one of these valves. One day a gentleman called on Captain Gordon in the cabin of his boat, and told him that he and twenty persons in his company were desirous of going on in his boat; "but," said the gentleman, "I can't do it, neither can my company; for I have been below examining your machinery, and I find you haven't got 'Evan's Patent Safety-Valve' attached to your engine. For this reason we can't go with you."

"I shall be very happy to have your company," said Captain Gordon. "Come below, and I will show you the best safety-valve in the world."

They walked down together to the engine-room. The captain stepped up to his sturdy engineer, and clapping him on the shoulder, said to the gentleman,—"There, sir, is my safety-valve—the best to be found anywhere;—a man who never drinks anything but PURE COLD WATER!"

"Your are right, captain," said the stranger; "I want no better safety-valve than that. We will come on board, sir."

Some years ago, a fine ship called the *Neptune*, with a crew of thirty-six men, sailed from the harbour of Aberdeen, in Scotland. It was early on a fine morning in May when she started, with the fairest prospect of good weather and of a prosperous voyage. Not long after she had gone the sky became cloudy. The wind changed. It came out directly ahead of the ship, and went on increasing in violence till it blew a furious gale. By and bye the *Neptune* was seen standing back towards the harbour, right before the wind, and with her sails set as though it was only blowing a fair, stiff breeze. She came bounding on before the storm like a maddened war-house. The tidings spread like lightning, and hundreds of people gathered on the pier to watch the strange sight. Something was wrong on board the ship. What COULD it be? The entrance to the harbour was very narrow, and beyond this were ledges of dangerous rocks. Over these the sea is now breaking in foam and thunder. Right on towards them the ship is hastening. What CAN be the matter? The people look on in silent horror. Now the ship rises on a mountain wave, and now she plunges into the foaming water. An attempt is made to shorten sails. It fails. She hastens on. A moment more, and hark! that thundering crash! The cry is heard—" SHE'S LOST !—SHE'S LOST !" She went to pieces. One man alone, of all on board, was saved. He lived to tell the dreadful secret. The giant was on

board of that vessel. The crew were all intoxicated, and could not manage the vessel.

Thus we see that, while cold water promotes
safety, there can be no safety where the giant
Intemperance is allowed to come. He is an enemy
to it.

And he is an enemy to HONOUR, too. You can
keep your honour if you keep to cold water.
But get into the habit of drinking liquor, and
your honour will soon be turned to shame. The
giant Intemperance has such a bad name among
men, that if you fall into his power your honour
is lost. Everything that is wicked, vile, and
shameful is associated with our thoughts of this
giant. And he makes his prisoners so much like
himself, that the same disgrace is fixed to their
names. So that no matter how honoured and
respected a man has been before, as soon as he
becomes a captive of this giant, he begins to lose
his honour.

Men do not like to be called DRUNKARDS. The
name is a mark of disgrace. It points them out
as prisoners of this giant. But every one who
drinks wine or liquor is in danger of becoming a
drunkard, and thus covering himself with shame
and dishonour.

Everything that is sinful should be considered

as a shame and disgrace. It's a shame for a man willingly to lose all his sense and reason, and act like a fool;—but this is what the drunkard does. It's a shame for a man to lose all proper feeling, and become as hard-hearted as a stone;—but this is what the drunkard does. It's a shame for a man to reel through the streets, and wallow in the gutter like a pig;—but this is what the drunkard does. It's a shame for a man to neglect his business, and spend his time in idleness; to leave his children beggars, and his wife a broken-hearted widow;—but this is what the drunkard does. It's a shame for a man to gamble, and rob, and murder, and commit all kinds of abominations;—but these are what the drunkard does.

Nearly all the people who live in our almshouses, who are sent to our penitentiaries, and brought to the gallows, are led there by drinking. And those who use intoxicating liquors at all, are in danger of being led into any or all of these evils. Or if not led into them themselves, they are in danger of leading others into them. The giant Intemperance carries danger and disgrace with him. If you would live in safety and honour, put as wide a space between yourself and him as possible;—drink nothing that intoxicates, but keep to pure cold water.

This, then, is the third reason why we should resist this giant—BECAUSE HE IS AN ENEMY TO SAFETY AND HONOUR.

CHAPTER X.

We should fight against this Giant BECAUSE HE IS AN ENEMY TO COMFORT AND HAPPINESS.

Several years ago, when Barnum's Museum was on the corner of Seventh and Chesnut Streets, Philadelphia, there was, in one of the rooms, a representation of a cold water drinker's home, and of a drunkard's home. These were placed side by side, so as to show the contrast more strongly. The figures were all of wax, and just about the size of living persons, so that it looked very real.

The first one represented a good-sized room, with a neat carpet on the floor, and pretty paper on the walls. Two or three pictures were hanging against the sides of the room. A cheerful fire was burning in the grate. In the centre of the room stood a table with a snow-white cloth upon it. A tidy, happy-looking lady was spreading some very inviting things for breakfast; while the largest of the children was bringing in a pitcher of water to fill the tumblers that were placed by every plate. An easy arm-chair was drawn up near the fire, and the father was leaning back in it, reading the morning paper, looking very snug and cosy in his wrapper and slippers. Around him a group of bright-eyed, rosy-cheeked little ones were playing, while a toddling boy was tugging at his father's gown, trying to climb up into his lap.

You did not need any one to tell you that comfort and happiness were there. Everything looked so pleasant, that one almost felt like opening the door and walking in to share their happiness. This was the cold water drinker's home.

Right next to it was the other scene. It was a room with bare floor, strewn with litter, and blackened with dirt. The plaster was falling from the walls and the ceiling. In the fire-place there were two or three half-burnt sticks smouldering. An old bedstead stood in the corner, and a few ragged coverlets lay tumbled in a heap upon it. The rest of the furniture consisted of a table, and one or two rickety chairs. A loaf of bread, partly cut, and a bottle on the table, were the only signs of a breakfast. The father, with his face unwashed, his beard unshaven, and his hair all tangled and matted, was beating a trembling child. The rest of the children were crowding up in the corner, pale and frightened, but each holding on to a dry crust of bread. Their faces were thin and sickly. The mother sat upon the bed, her head between her hands, and her hair streaming wildly over her shoulders. Thin and tattered rags were the only clothes any of them had on. Misery and wretchedness were as plainly seen there as if written with a sunbeam. This was the drunkard's home.

Children, which is the pleasantest picture? Which would you rather should be your home?

All the difference was made by the PITCHER and the BOTTLE. The water in that pitcher had kept the giant Intemperance away from the first home; while the rum in the bottle had brought him into the other one. And it was because HE was there that all was so wretched. He always drives comfort and happiness out from every house he enters. He turns gladness into sorrow, smiles into sighs, laughter into tears, wherever he goes. He makes his prisoners miserable themselves, and all about them unhappy, too. Mothers and fathers, wives and children, brothers and sisters, suffer wherever he comes.

Let me tell you of a mother's sorrow, occasioned by a drunken son;—and of a whole family's sorrow, occasioned by a drunken husband and father.

A company of southern ladies, assembled in a parlour, were one day talking about their different troubles. Each one had something to say about her own trials. But there was one in the company, pale and sad looking, who for a while said nothing. Suddenly rousing herself at last, she said :—

"My friends, you don't any of you know what trouble is."

"Will you please, Mrs Gray," said the kind voice of one who knew her story, "tell the ladies what you call trouble?"

"I will, if you desire it; for, in the words of the prophet, 'I am the one who hath seen affliction.'

"My parents were very well off, and my girl-hood was surrounded by all the comforts of life. Every wish of my heart was gratified, and I was cheerful and happy.

"At the age of nineteen I married one whom I loved more than all the world besides. Our home was retired; but the sun never shone upon a lovelier spot or a happier household. Years rolled on peacefully. Five lovely children sat around our table, and a little curly head still nestled in my bosom. One night, about sundown, one of those fierce black storms came on which are so common to our southern climate. For many hours the rain poured down incessantly. Morning dawned, but still the elements raged. The country around us was overflowed. The little stream near our dwelling became a foaming torrent. Before we were aware of it, our house was surrounded by water. I managed, with my babe, to reach a little elevated spot where the thick foliage of a few wide-spreading trees afforded some protection, while my husband and sons strove to save what they could of our property. At last a fearful surge swept away my husband, and he never rose again. Ladies, no one ever loved a husband more; but THAT was not trouble.

"Presently my sons saw their danger, and the struggle for life became the only consideration. They were as brave, loving boys as ever blessed a mother's heart; and I watched their efforts to escape with such agony as only mothers can feel. They were so far off that I could not speak to them; but I could see them closing nearer and nearer to each other, as their little island grew smaller and smaller.

"The swollen river raged fearfully around the huge trees. Dead branches, upturned trunks, wrecks of houses, drowning cattle, and masses of rubbish, all went floating past us. My boys waved their hands to me, and then pointed upwards. I knew it was their farewell signal; and you, mothers, can imagine my anguish. I saw them perish;—ALL perish. Yet that was not trouble.

"I hugged my baby close to my heart; and when the water rose to my feet, I climbed into the low branches of the tree, and so kept retiring before it, till the hand of God stayed the waters that they should rise no further. I was saved. All my wordly possessions were swept away; all my earthly hopes blighted. Yet THAT was not trouble.

"My baby was all I had left on earth. I laboured day and night to support him and myself, and sought to train him in the right way; but as he grew older, evil companions won him away from me. He ceased to care for his mother's counsels; he would sneer at her kind entreaties and agonising prayers. HE BECAME FOND OF DRINKING. He left my humble roof that he might be unrestrained in his evil ways. And at last, one night, when heated by wine, he took the life of a fellow-creature. He ended his days upon the gallows! God had filled my cup of sorrow before; now it ran over. THAT was trouble, my friends, such as I hope the Lord in mercy may spare you from ever knowing!"

Boys, girls, can you bear to think that you might bring such sorrow on your dear father and mother? If you would not, be on your guard against the giant Intemperance. Let wine and liquors alone. Never touch them. That was a mother's sorrow.

Let us look at the sorrow brought on a family by the same dreadful evil.

Let me tell you an "old man's story."

Many years ago, a temperance meeting was held in a certain village. A little boy, who lived in the village, was very anxious to go, and persuaded his father to take him. The boy never forgot that meeting, and he wrote the account of it years afterwards. One of the speakers at the meeting was an old man. His hair was white, and his brow furrowed with age and sorrow. When he arose to speak he said:—

"My friends, I am an old man, standing alone at the end of life's journey. Tears are in my eyes, and deep sorrow is in my heart. I am without friends, or home, or kindred on earth. It was not always so. Once I had a mother. With her old heart crushed with sorrow she went down to her grave. I once had a wife;—a fair,

angel-hearted creature as ever smiled in an earthly
home. Her blue eye grew dim as the floods of
sorrow washed away its brightness; and her tender
heart I wrung till every fibre was broken. I
once had a noble boy; but he was driven from
the ruins of his home, and my old heart yearns
to know if he yet lives. I once had a babe, a
sweet, lovely babe; but these hands destroyed it,
and now it lives with Him who loveth the little
ones. Do not spurn me, my friends," continued
the old man. "There is light in my evening sky.
The spirit of my mother rejoices over the return
of her prodigal son. The injured wife smiles upon
him who turns back again to virtue and honour.
The child-angel visits me at nightfall, and I seem
to feel his tiny hands upon my feverish cheek.
My brave boy, if he yet lives, would forgive the
sorrowing old man for treatment that drove him
out into the world, and the blow that maimed
him for life. God forgive me for the ruin I
have brought upon all that were about me.

"I was a drunkard. From wealth and re-
spectability I plunged into poverty and shame.
I dragged my family down with me. For years
I saw the cheek of my wife grow pale, and
her step grow weary. I left her alone to struggle
for the children, while I was drinking and

rioting at the tavern. She never complained, though she and the children often went hungry to bed.

"One New-Year's night I returned late to the hut where charity had given us shelter. My wife was still up, and shivering over the coals. I demanded food. She told me there was none, and then burst into tears. I fiercely ordered her to get some. She turned her eyes sadly upon me, the tears falling fast over her pale cheek. At this moment the child in its cradle awoke and uttered a cry of hunger, startling the despairing mother, and making new sorrow in her breaking heart.

" 'We have no food, James;—we have had none for several days. I have nothing for the babe. Oh! my once kind husband, must we starve?'

"That sad, pleading face, and those streaming eyes, and the feeble wail of the child, maddened me;—and I—yes I, struck her a fierce blow in the face, and she fell forward upon the hearth. It seemed as if the furies of hell were raging in my bosom; and the feeling of the wrong I had committed added fuel to the flames. I had never struck my wife before, but now some terrible impulse drove me on, and I stooped down, as well as I could in my drunken state, and clenched both my hands in her hair.

"'For mercy's sake, James!' exclaimed my wife as she looked up into my fiendish countenance,— 'You will not kill us; you will not harm Willie?' and she sprang to the cradle and grasped him in her arms. I caught her again by the hair and dragged her to the door, and as I lifted the latch, the wind burst in with a cloud of snow. With a fiendish yell I still dragged her on, and hurled her out amid the darkness and storm. Then, with a wild laugh, I closed the door and fastened it. Her pleading moans and the sharp cry of her babe mingled with the wail of the blast. But my horrible work was not yet complete.

"I turned to the bed where my oldest son was lying, snatched him from his slumbers, and against his half awakened struggles, opened the door and thrust him out. In the agony of fear he uttered that sacred name I was no longer worthy to bear. He called me—FATHER! and locked his fingers in my side-pocket. I could not wrench that grasp away; but, with the cruelty of a fiend, I shut the door upon his arm, and, seizing my knife, severed it at the wrist.

"It was morning when I awoke, and the storm had ceased. I looked round to the accustomed place for my wife. As I missed her, a dim, dark scene, as of some horrible nightmare, came over

me. I thought it must be a fearful dream, but
involuntarily opened the outside door with a
shuddering dread. As the door opened the snow
burst in, and something fell across the threshold
with a dull, heavy sound. My blood shot like
melted lava through my veins, and I covered my
eyes to shut out the sight. It was—O God!
how horrible!—it was my own loving wife and
her babe, frozen to death! With true mother's
love she had bowed herself over the child to
shield it, and wrapped all her clothing around it,
leaving her own person exposed to the storm.
She had placed her hair over the face of the
child, and the sleet had frozen it to the pale
cheek. The frost was white on the lids of its
half-opened eyes and upon its tiny fingers.

"I never knew what became of my brave boy."

Here the old man bowed his head and wept;
and all in the house wept with him. Then, in
the low tones of heart-broken sorrow, he concluded:—

"I was arrested, and for long months I was
a raving maniac. When I recovered I was
sentenced to the penitentiary for ten years; but
this was nothing to the tortures I have endured
in my own bosom. And now I desire to spend
the little remnant of my life in striving to

warn others not to enter a path which has been so dark and fearful to me."

When the old man had finished, the temperance pledge was produced, and he asked the people to come forward and sign it. The boy of the father referred to leaped from his seat, and pressed forward to sign the pledge. As he took the pen in hand he hesitated a moment.

"Sign it, young man, sign it," said the venerable speaker. "Angels would sign it. I would write my name in blood ten thousand times if it would undo the ruin I have wrought, and bring back my loved and lost ones."

The young man wrote,—" Mortimer Hudson." The old man looked. He wiped his eyes and looked again. His face flushed with fiery red, and then a death-like paleness came over it.

"It is—no, it cannot be;—yet how strange!" he muttered. "Pardon me, sir, but that was the name of my brave boy."

The young man trembled, and held up his left arm from which the hand had been severed.

They looked for a moment in each other's eyes; and the old man exclaimed:—

"My own injured boy!"

The young man cried out!—

"My poor, dear father!"

Then they fell upon each other's neck and wept, till it seemed as if their souls would mingle into one.

Thus we see the misery and wretchedness this fearful giant Intemperance brings upon the drunkard and upon all his family. If you love those at home, make up your minds that YOU will never cause them such sorrow and shame. Keep everything that intoxicates from your lips, and you will keep the giant from your home. Do so BECAUSE HE IS AN ENEMY TO COMFORT AND HAPPINESS.

Those of you who have read ancient history remember Hannibal, the great Carthaginian general. The Romans were the enemies of the Carthaginians. Hannibal's father had been general for many years, and had fought many battles against the Romans. He wanted his son to feel that they were his enemies, and that he must begin early to fight them. So, one day, when Hannibal was about nine years old, his father gathered all the soldiers together. Then he went into his tent and led out little Hannibal, and took him to the large altar where they used to offer sacrifices to their gods. Upon this altar he made him place his hand, and, in the presence of the whole army, swear that as long as he lived he would

be an enemy to the Romans, and that he would
fight against them with all his power.

Hannibal never forgot that promise. He became
the greatest enemy the Romans ever had.

Now, my dear children, you have a great many
enemies. All these giants that we have been
talking about are your enemies. They want to
capture you, and they will try hard to do it.
They are all strong and fierce. But the last one,
the giant Intemperance, is the greatest enemy to
you of them all. And he is the strongest and
most cruel of all. The sooner you feel this,
the sooner you will be on your guard against
him, and the more you will learn to hate him.
And so I want you to do what Hannibal did.
I want you to determine, NOW, while you are
young, that as long as you live, you will be
an enemy of this giant, and fight against
him with all your power. I want you to
VOW LIFE-LONG WAR against him! Never make
peace with him! Never give him any quarter!

I do not ask you to sign a pledge, but I
do ask you all to resolve solemnly, that, by
the help of God, you will never allow yourselves to drink wine or liquor of any kind
unless you are sick, and it is given by the
physician as a medicine. "TOUCH NOT—TASTE

NOT—HANDLE   NOT." This   is   the   only   safe
course.

Those who do not follow this rule often fall
into the power of the giant Intemperance very
suddenly, and when they least expect it; and,
though they may escape again, do things while
they are his prisoners that lead them into great
trouble.

A man named John Cafree was shot in a fire-
man's quarrel in this city some time ago. The
man who shot him was not an habitual drunkard.
He was generally a sober, industrious man. But
on that occasion he was tempted to drink too
much, and now the dreadful guilt of murder is
resting upon him.

Some years since there was a crowd gathered
round a gallows to see a young man hung. The
sheriff took out his watch and said:—"If you
have anything to say, speak now, for you have
only five minutes to live." The young man burst
into tears and said:—"Alas! and must I die?
I had only one little brother. He had beautiful
blue eyes and flaxen hair, and I loved him. But
one day I got drunk for the first and only time
in my life. On coming home I found my brother
gathering strawberries in the garden. Without any
sufficient cause I became angry with him, and

struck him a blow with an iron rake. That blow killed him. I knew nothing about what was done till the next morning. On awakening from sleep I found myself tied and guarded; and was told that when my little brother was discovered he was dead, and his hair was clotted with blood and brains. Drinking liquor has done it. THAT has ruined me. I never was drunk but once, and now I am to hang for it. I have only one word more to say, and then I am going to stand before my Judge. I wish to say to young people— Never, never, never touch anything that can intoxicate." As he spoke these words he sprung from the scaffold and was launched into eternity.

My dear boys, remember this warning. "Never touch anything that can intoxicate." And my dear girls, do you remember it too. Don't think that because you are females you are in no danger. You ARE in danger.

In New York they are building a house for habitual drunkards, where they can be treated as sick or insane people are. Since this building has been started, nearly three thousand confirmed drunkards have applied for admission. Among these are between FOUR AND FIVE HUNDRED FEMALES FROM THE MOST RESPECTABLE FAMILIES. ALL persons who drink wine, or liquor AT ALL, are in danger both of becoming drunkards themselves, and of making others drunkards by their example. Drink cold water and you are in no danger. The giant Intemperance will never be able to make you his prisoner if you keep to cold water.

Now, how many giants have we spoken of? Five. What was the first? The GIANT HEATHEN-ISM. How are we to fight him? BY THROWING THE STONES OF TRUTH AT HIM. What was the second? THE GIANT SELFISHNESS. How are we to fight him? BY SELF-DENIAL. What was the third? THE GIANT COVETOUSNESS. How are we to fight him? BY LEARNING TO GIVE. What was the fourth? THE GIANT ILL-TEMPER. How are we to fight him? BY LEARNING TO BE LIKE JESUS. What was the fifth? THE GIANT INTEMPERANCE. And how are we to fight him? BY DRINKING COLD WATER. We had four good reasons why we should fight this giant. What are they? We ought to fight him because COLD WATER IS THE DRINK THAT GOD HAS MADE FOR US; BECAUSE HE IS AN ENEMY TO HEALTH AND STRENGTH; TO SAFETY AND HONOUR; TO COMFORT AND HAPPINESS.

In conclusion, my dear children, I want you all to become brave giant fighters. Fighting in general is poor business. For men and women, or boys and girls, to be fighting among themselves is a

shameful thing. But to be fighting these giants
is very different. This is proper for girls as well
as boys; for ladies as well as gentlemen. It is a
right thing, a brave thing, an honourable thing.
But do not try to fight them in your own strength,
or else you are sure to be beaten. David prayed
to God to help him when he became a giant
fighter. It was this which made him successful.
And you must do the same. Pray for Jesus to
help you. Then go at the giants with all your
might, and He will "teach your hands to war,
and your fingers to fight;" and will bring you off
at last, " conquerors, and more than conquerors."

The Good Soldiers.

"Good soldiers of Jesus Christ."—2 TIMOTHY ii. 3.

THERE is a great deal said in the Bible about soldiers. The Church of Jesus Christ — made up of all the people who love Him — is compared in one place to "an army with banners," Cant. vi. 4. Our blessed Saviour is spoken of as "the leader or commander" of this army, Isa. lv. 4. And in one place in the New Testament, St. Paul calls Jesus "the Captain of our salvation," Heb. ii. 10. And in the verse in which our text is found, He calls on all who are trying to be true Christians to "endure hardness as good soldiers of Jesus Christ."

Now, the one great object we have in view in our Sunday-school work, is that all our scholars should become Christians. And every true Christian is a soldier of Jesus Christ. Perhaps some of the girls may think, "Well, this subject does not suit us. We do not want to be soldiers." That is true. We do not want our dear daughters and sisters to wear swords and shoulder muskets, and go out to fight for their country in the time of war. But then we do want you all to be the "soldiers of Jesus Christ." If you become Christians, this is just what you will be. Some of the best and bravest soldiers that Jesus has ever had have been female soldiers. And so this subject suits the girls as well as the boys. And now the question before us is, *How may we become good soldiers of Jesus Christ?* I wish to speak of three things that are necessary if we wish to learn this lesson.

In the first place, to become good soldiers of Jesus Christ, WE MUST WEAR THE UNIFORM *of Christ.*

The soldier's uniform is the dress that he wears. This is often very beautiful. Sometimes the uniform is of a blue colour, sometimes it is grey or scarlet. Sometimes it is all of one colour, while at other times it is made up of a variety of different colours. To see a whole regiment of men all dressed in the same uniform, and keeping step together, is a very pleasing sight.

But the uniform which the soldiers of Jesus wear is not the dress that is put upon their bodies, but the dress that is put upon their souls. This uniform is not made up of different-coloured cloth, such as we see other soldiers wear. No;

but it is made up of the tempers, or dispositions, which form their character.

To wear the uniform of Jesus, then, is to have the same mind, or spirit, or temper that He had. And the Bible tells us that, unless we have the mind or spirit of Jesus, we cannot be His servants or followers.

Now, let us see what sort of a mind or spirit Jesus had, and then we can tell whether we are wearing the uniform of Jesus or not.

The spirit of Jesus was a *gentle* spirit; this is part of the uniform of Jesus. And if we want to be good soldiers of Jesus, we must wear this uniform. We must try to be gentle.

We never hear that Jesus spoke a cross or angry word. Sometimes He spoke severely to the people about their sins, but He was never cross. The Jews were very unkind to Him; they told stories about Him; they called Him bad names. But He never spoke back to them in the same way; He never threatened them or stormed at them. He came as God's Lamb to be sacrificed for us, and He was as gentle and mild as a lamb. And we cannot be good soldiers of Jesus Christ, unless we wear this part of His uniform, and try to be gentle as He was. But if we do wear this uniform, we shall be very useful.

An old gentleman once lived in a large house. He had plenty of money, and servants, and everything he wanted, and yet he was not happy—he was not gentle. When things did not just please him, he would get cross, and speak sharply. His servants all left him, and he was in great trouble. Quite discouraged, he went to a neighbour's to tell him of his difficulties. This man was "a good soldier of Jesus Christ." He was wearing the uniform of gentleness. After listening to his neighbour's story, he said to him—

"It seems to me, my friend, it would be well for you to *oil yourself a little.*"

"To oil myself! What do you mean?"

"Let me explain. Some time ago one of the doors in our house had a creaking hinge. It made such a disagreeable noise whenever it was opened or shut, that nobody cared to touch it. One day I oiled its hinges, and since then we have had no trouble with it."

"And so you think I'm like a creaking hinge, do you?" said the neighbour. "Pray, how do you want me to oil myself?"

"It's easy enough to tell that," said his friend. "Go home and engage a servant. If he does well, praise him for it. If he doesn't do just as you would like, don't get cross and scold him. Soften

your voice and words with the oil of love and
gentleness, and you will not have much trouble."

That was good advice. If we are good soldiers
of Jesus, we must carry this precious oil with us,
and use it all the time. Gentleness is part of the
uniform of Jesus. Let us try to wear this.

But the spirit of Jesus was *a forgiving spirit.*
This is another part of His uniform that we must
wear, if we wish to be good soldiers of Jesus.

Such a spirit of forgiveness as Jesus showed
was never seen in our world before or since. The
Jews persecuted Him, and put Him to death in
a very cruel way, by nailing Him to the cross,
although He had never done anything but good
to them all His days. And yet, while He hung
suffering on the cross, Jesus did not feel angry
towards them. He spoke no harsh, cross words
to them. But He felt pity for them. He prayed
for them, and said, "Father, forgive them, for they
know not what they do!" How wonderful this
was! What a forgiving spirit Jesus had! This
was the uniform He wore. And we must wear
it too, if we would be "good soldiers of Jesus
Christ."

The superintendent of a Sunday-school was standing at his window one day. He saw two of the
girls belonging to his school going by. They had

evidently had a quarrel with some acquaintance. One of them was saying to the other, in a very angry voice—

" Sally, I tell you what; if I were in your place I'd never speak to her again. I'd be mad at her as long as I lived."

The superintendent listened very anxiously to hear what Sally would say to this. He felt greatly relieved when she said—

" No, Lou, I wouldn't do so for all the world. You know we must try and be like Jesus. I'm going to forgive and forget as soon as I can, and try to make her love me. This is what Jesus would have done."

There you see the uniform of Christ. That dear girl was a good soldier of Jesus Christ. She had a forgiving spirit.

And then the spirit of Jesus was a *trusting* spirit. He felt sure that His Father was always with Him, and would never let anything hurt Him. Even when His enemies had taken Him, and were going to crucify Him, He said that if He should ask His Father, He would send legions of angels to deliver Him out of their hands. And this is just the feeling that He wants us to have. If we are the soldiers of Jesus, and are trying to love and serve Him, He will always be with us.

He will watch over us and take care of us, and so we never need be afraid. Let me tell you about a little girl who had this trusting spirit.

She was only four years old, and was called Birdie. She had been taught that God loved her, and always took care of her.

One day there was a heavy thunder-storm, and Birdie's sisters, and even her mamma, laid by their sewing, and drew their chairs into the middle of the room. They were pale and trembling with fear. But Birdie stood close by the window, watching the storm with great interest.

"Oh, mamma, ain't that bu'ful?" she cried, clapping her hands with delight, as a vivid flash of lightning burst from the black clouds, and the thunder pealed and rattled overhead.

"It's God's voice, Birdie," said mamma, and her own voice trembled.

"He talks velly loud, don't He, mamma? S'pose it's so as deaf Aunt Betsy can hear, and uver deaf folks."

"Oh, Birdie, dear, come straight away from that window," said her sister Nellie, whose face was all white with fear.

"*What for?*" asked Birdie.

"Oh! because the lightning is so sharp, and it thunders so loud."

But Birdie shook her head, and, looking over her shoulder with a happy smile on her face, lisped out,—

"If it funders, let it funder! It's God that makes it funder, and He'll take care of me. I ain't a bit afraid to hear God talk, sister Nellie." That was beautiful. Birdie was a good soldier of Jesus Christ. She had a trusting spirit. This is part of the uniform of Jesus. The spirit of Jesus is a gentle spirit, a forgiving spirit, a trusting spirit. These help to make up the uniform of Jesus. The first thing for us to do, if we would be good soldiers of Jesus, is to wear the uniform of Jesus.

The second thing for us to do, if we would be good soldiers of Jesus Christ, is to—OBEY THE ORDERS OF JESUS.

The most important thing for a soldier to do is to learn to obey. No matter how hard or dangerous the thing is that he is told to do, there is no choice left him, but just to go and do it. He may be perfectly sure that he will be killed in trying to do it. That makes no difference. He must obey. It is impossible to be a good soldier without learning this lesson.

Many years ago, the great battle of Waterloo was fought in Europe, between the English and

the French.   The Duke of Wellington commanded
the English army, and the Emperor Napoleon
Bonaparte commanded the French.   In the midst
of the battle, the French made a furious attack
on a particular part of the English lines.   It was
very important that the English soldiers should
stand their ground then, and hold that point.
The success of the battle depended on it.   Courier
after courier came dashing into the presence of
the Duke of Wellington.   They asked him to send
reinforcements to that part of the field, or to order
the troops away from it, or else they would be
compelled to retreat from the fierce onsets of the
French.   By all these messengers the Duke sent
back the same order,—" Stand firm."

"We shall all perish," said one of the officers.
"Stand firm," was still the Duke's answer.   "You'll
find us all there when the battle's over," said the
officer, and galloped back to his post to die.   And
it turned out just as he had said.   Not one of
that gallant brigade left his post.   And not one
was living when the battle was over.   They
obeyed their orders.   They "stood firm."   But
they all died in doing it.   Those were good
soldiers.   They had learned to obey orders.

Some time ago, a large ship was going from
England to the East Indies.   She was carrying a

regiment of soldiers. When they were about half-way through their voyage, the vessel sprang a leak, and began to fill with water. The lifeboats were launched and made ready, but there were not enough of them to save all on board the ship. Only the officers of the ship, the cabin passengers, and some of the crew, could be taken in the boats. The soldiers had to be left on board, to go down with the ship. The officers determined to die with their men. The colonel was afraid the men would get unruly if they had nothing to do. That he might prevent this, he ordered them to prepare for parade. Soon they all appeared in full dress. He set the regimental band on the quarter-deck, with orders to keep on playing lively airs. Then he formed his men in close ranks on the deck. With his sword drawn in his hand, he took his place at their head. Every officer and man is at his post. The vessel is gradually sinking; but they stand steady at their post, each man keeping step. And then, just as the vessel is settling for its last plunge, and death is rushing in upon them, the colonel cries,—" Present arms!" and that whole regiment of brave men go down into their watery grave, presenting arms as death approached them.

Those were good soldiers. They had learned

to obey orders. But this is a hard lesson to learn.

I heard, some time ago, of a German captain who found it difficult to teach his men this lesson. He was drilling a company of volunteers. The parade-ground was a field near the seaside. The men were going through their exercises very nicely. But the captain thought he would give them a lesson about obeying orders. They were marching up and down, in the line of the water, at some distance from it. He concluded to give them an order to march directly towards the water, and see how far they would go. The men are marching along. "Halt, company!" says the captain. In a moment they halt. "Right face!" is the next word, and instantly they wheel round. "Forwards, march!" is the next order. At once they begin to march directly towards the water. On they go, nearer and nearer to it. Soon they reach the edge of the water. Then there is a sudden halt. "Vat for you shtop? I no say halt," cried the captain.

"Why, captain, here's the water," said one of the men.

"Vell, vat of it?" cried he, greatly excited, "Vater is notting. Fire is notting. Everyting is notting. Ven I say 'Forwards, march!' den you *must* 'forwards, march.'"

The captain was right. The first duty of a soldier is to learn to obey. If we want to be good soldiers of Jesus, we must learn to obey His orders.

Several boys were playing marbles. In the midst of their sport it began to rain. One of the boys, named Freddie, stopped and said, " Boys, I must go home. Mother told me not to stay out in the rain."

"Your mother—fudge !" said two or three of the boys. "The rain won't hurt you any more than it will us." Freddie turned on them with a look of pity, and yet with the courage of a hero, while he calmly said, "*I'll not disobey my mother for any of you.*"

That was the spirit of a good soldier.

After a great battle once, the general was talking to his officers about the events of the day. He asked them who had done the best that day. Some spoke of one man who had fought very bravely, and some of another.

"No," said the general, "you are all mistaken. The best man in the field to-day was a soldier who was just lifting up his arms to strike an enemy, but when he heard the trumpet sound a retreat, he checked himself, and dropped his arm without striking the blow. That perfect and

ready obedience to the will of his general is the
noblest thing that has been done to-day."

One of the best illustrations I ever heard of
the way in which we ought to learn to obey God,
was given once by a negro preacher, when speaking on this point. He said,—"Bredren, whatever
de good Lord tell me to do in dis blessed book,
dat I'm gwine to do. If I see in it dat I must
jump froo' a stone wall, I'm gwine to jump.
Gettin' froo' it 'longs to God. Jumpin' at it 'longs
to me."

That is the true spirit of a soldier.

And this is the spirit that we must have, if we
want to be "good soldiers of Jesus Christ."

We must obey the orders of Jesus. This is the
second thing for good soldiers of Jesus to do.

*But there is a third thing for us to do, in order
to be good soldiers of Jesus; we must*—FOLLOW
THE EXAMPLE OF JESUS.

Jesus came into our world, not only to die for
our sins, and to show us by His teaching how we
ought to live, but He came to do one other thing.
This was a very important thing. He came to
leave us an example that we might safely follow.
The apostle tells us that Jesus has "left us an
example that we should follow His steps" (1 Peter
ii. 21). The example of Jesus is the only perfect

example that we can find. The best people in the world do wrong some time; and so, if we follow their example, we cannot always be sure it is right. But Jesus never did, or said, or thought, or felt anything that was wrong. We can follow His example safely. We never need have a moment's fear about going wrong when we are treading in His steps.

And Jesus wants us to follow His . example, because He knows that example is more powerful than words.

When Alexander the Great was leading his army over some mountains once, they found their way all stopped up with ice and snow. His soldiers were tired out with hard marching, and so disheartened with the difficulties before them, that they halted. It seemed as if they would rather lie down and die than try to go on any farther. When Alexander saw this, he did not begin to scold the men, and storm at them. Instead of this, he got down from his horse, laid aside his cloak, took up a pickaxe, and, without saying a word to anyone, went quietly to work, digging away at the ice. As soon as the officers saw this, they did the same. The men looked on in surprise for a few moments, and then, forgetting how tired they were, they went to work with a will,

and pretty soon they got through all their difficulties.   Those were good soldiers, because they
followed the example of their leader.

When the native converts in the island of Madagascar used to come to the missionaries and want
to be baptized, it often happened that questions
like these would be put to them: "What was it that
first led you to think of becoming Christians ?
Was it some sermon you heard, or something that
was read from the Bible ?"

In many cases the answer would be, "No, it was
not any particular sermon, or passage from the
Bible; but it was the example of those who had
become Christians, that led us to think seriously
about these things.   We knew such an one who
used to be a thief another who was a drunkard,
and another who was very cruel and unkind to
his family.   But now they are all changed.   The
thief has become an honest man, the drunkard is
sober and respectable, and the man of bad temper
has become gentle and kind in his home.   There
must be something in a religion that can work
such changes as these."

You see that those Madagascar Christians were
good soldiers of Jesus.   They were following His
example. In this way they were doing more good
than even the missionaries did with their preaching.

"I say, Jim," said Harry to his brother, "didn't you feel mad, at noon to-day, when mother kept us waiting half an hour for our dinner?"

"Well, Harry, I must confess I was a little restive at first, for I was as hungry as an alligator; but I held the lamp to my feet, and thought of my Captain."

"What do you mean by your lamp and your Captain?" asked Harry.

"The Bible is the lamp I'm trying to use," said Jim. "You know we read, 'Thy word is a lamp unto my feet, and a light unto my path.' And what's the good of having a lamp, unless we use it to show us how to walk? When I felt like getting mad, I thought of the words, 'He that ruleth his spirit is better than he that taketh a city.' And then I said to myself, 'How would Jesus act if he were in my place?' You know the Bible tells us that Jesus is 'the Captain of our salvation.' I want to be a good soldier of Jesus. To do this, I must follow His example. So I prayed for grace to rule my own spirit, and follow the example of Jesus. This is what I mean, Harry," said Jim, "by holding the lamp to my feet, and thinking of my Captain."

Now Jim had the real spirit of a soldier. He was trying to follow the example of Jesus. And

this is what we must do, if we want to be "good
soldiers of Jesus Christ."

I will only give you one other illustration of
the way in which we must follow the example of
Jesus, and of the good we can do in this way.

This story is about a young man who was a
sailor. He was an excellent sailor, and a good
Christian man. He had first gone to sea as a
sailor boy, but had risen by degrees, till he occupied the position of first mate or chief officer on
board a large ship that sailed from Boston. The
young man's name was Palmer. Once when the
vessel in which Mr. Palmer sailed came home to
Boston, there was a change of captains. The old
captain resigned, and a new one was appointed to
command the ship. When a captain takes charge
of a ship, he always likes to choose his own first
mate, and generally he is allowed to do so. But
in this case the owners of the ship insisted that
Mr. Palmer should remain on board as the first
mate. The captain was obliged to give way to
them. This made him very angry, and he determined to do everything he could to make Mr.
Palmer's position on board the ship as uncomfort-
able as possible. And he certainly did this. He
crossed him whenever he could. He found fault
with everything he did. He took every chance

he could get of showing him disrespect before the crew, and tried to hurt his feelings in every possible way. But Palmer was a noble, Christian young man, and tried to follow the example of his Saviour. Yet he found it very hard.

Many a time on the voyage he said to himself, "There's no use talking about it; I can't stand this, and I won't." Then he would think, "Jesus, my Master, would stand it, if He were in my place;" and this thought would lead him to overlook the captain's bad treatment, and try to do his duty in the best way he could.

The ship was on a trading voyage, which was to last for two years, and Palmer had shipped for the voyage. He felt that it would be a hard trial to go on, bearing all this so long. At every port they came to, he almost made up his mind to quit the ship. "But no," he said, "Jesus, when He was reviled, reviled not again; I will bear and forbear for His sake. I'll stand the voyage through." And so he did. Instead of paying "tit for tat," or answering crossly when he was crossly spoken to, he returned meekness and forgiveness for insult. He was always respectful to the surly old commander, and never neglected any of his duties. And so he kept on till the close of the voyage.

But at last the voyage ended. The ship came

back to Boston. Then he made up his mind to quit at once. But just as he was leaving the ship, the captain called him into his state-room, and, stretching out his hand to him, frankly said,—

"Mr. Palmer, I beg your pardon for all my bad conduct to you. I've treated you like a dog, and you have always behaved like a gentleman. I'm ashamed of myself, and so I ought to be. I was angry because I couldn't have my own mate; but you have been too much for me. I used to think that there was nothing in religion, but now I know there is. Your sort of spirit I've not been used to; it's beat me,"—and tears came into the captain's eyes,—" it's fairly beat me. I've not heard many sermons, but you've preached me one two years long, and it's cured me of my mistake about religion. I used to think my old mate was a good one, but you are the best mate I ever had. I can't part with you, Mr. Palmer: I want you for the next voyage, and I'll try to make amends for my past conduct."

Mr. Palmer went with him. The captain treated him as kindly as though he had been his own son. At the end of that voyage the captain left the ship, and recommended the owners to make Mr. Palmer captain. They did so, and a first-rate captain he made.

Now that honest sailor was a good soldier of Jesus Christ. He followed the example of Jesus, and we see how much good he did in that way.

Let us all try to be good soldiers of Jesus Christ. Remember the three things that we must do, if we want to be His soldiers.

We *must wear the uniform of Jesus.* We *must obey the orders of Jesus.* We *must follow the example of Jesus.* We cannot do any of these things in our own strength; but if we pray to Jesus for His grace, He will help us to "fight manfully under His banner, and continue His faithful soldiers and servants unto our life's end."

The Conqueror's Jewel.

"*An agate.*"—Exod. xxviii. 19.

THIS precious stone was regarded in old times as the conqueror's jewel. It was supposed that if a person carried one of these jewels about with him, he would be sure to be successful in anything that he undertook. In every conflict with evil, it would give him the victory. This conqueror's jewel we may consider as representing the grace of God. When we are called upon to fight against evil in any form, it is only the grace of God that can make us conquerors. The greatest enemy with which we have to fight is sin. This enemy meets us in many forms. But the form in which it gives us more trouble than any other, is perhaps that of selfishness. This is an evil that is very hard to conquer.

Suppose we are walking in the country, and meet a snake in the path; with the cane in our hand we strike it again and again, till it lies still and motionless. We leave it, and go on our way, feeling sure that we have killed the snake. But

when we have finished our walk, and come back
to the place where we left the snake, we find it
still alive and active.   Then we say to ourselves,
"Snakes are hard to kill."   And it is just so with
selfishness.   It is a very difficult thing to conquer
it.   If we wish to subdue it, and get the victory
over it, we must be sure to have this conqueror's
jewel, the grace of God.   And there are three
things that this jewel will lead us to do in fighting against selfishness.

In the first place, it will lead us—TO PRAY
AGAINST IT.

Prayer is necessary to our success in everything
we do.   Jesus said to His disciples, "Without me
ye can do nothing."   And this is as true now as
it was then.   It is as true of us as it was of
the disciples.   And it is particularly true of the
thing we are now considering.   If we want to get
the victory over the selfishness of our own hearts,
it is especially necessary for us to pray to Jesus
to help us.

Here is an illustration, in a story of two boys
who tried to get the victory over themselves in
this way.   These boys were brothers.   One of
them was named Henry, and the other Martin.
Henry was quick and passionate, while Martin was
sullen and dogged in his disposition.   They often

quarrelled together, and sometimes about the merest
trifles.   Yet their mother was a good Christian
woman, and tried to show them how wrong it was
to give way to their bad tempers.   And the boys
really wanted to do better, but they did not seem
to know how.   Henry, the oldest, was at a boarding-school.   Christmas was coming, when he expected to go home to spend his vacation.   He was
very anxious to have a pleasant visit at home
during the holidays, but he knew that if he and
Martin got to quarrelling, as they generally did, it
would spoil all their pleasure.   So he wrote to his
brother, some time before the close of the session,
telling him that he hoped they should be able to
get along more peaceably and pleasantly together,
and suggesting a new plan for subduing their bad
tempers, and getting the victory over themselves.

Martin received Henry's letter very kindly, and
agreed at once to adopt his plan ; for he really
wanted to be a good boy, and felt ashamed to
think that two brothers could not live in their
own home without quarrelling.

Well, the vacation time came.   Henry arrived
at home, and the holidays were passing away very
pleasantly.   Their mother was delighted to see how
nicely the boys were getting on together.   One
day she told Henry how glad she was to see the

great change which had taken place in himself
and Martin.

"Yes, mother," said Henry, "we have felt a great
deal happier, and have got on much more comfort-
ably, since we have tried our new plan."

"Your new plan! What do you mean by that?"
she asked, with surprise.

" Why, you see we have agreed to pray earnestly,
every day, that God would help us not to give
way to our bad tempers, and to get the victory
over ourselves."—This was what Henry had written
to Martin about before he came home at vacation.
—"And then, besides praying," said Henry, "Martin
has written down on a piece of paper a number of
texts of Scripture about temper.   We each carry
one of these pieces of paper in our pocket, and
when I am tempted to be cross, or he is tempted
to be sulky, we take out our paper and read it,
and in this way we feel that God is helping us
very much.   Here is my paper, mother;" and then
Henry took it out and read these verses:—

"Little children, love one another."

"Let not the sun go down upon your wrath."

"Leave off contention before it be meddled
with."

"Be slow to speak, slow to wrath."

"Overcome evil with good."

"Bless them which persecute you; bless, and curse not."

"Let brotherly love continue."

"Be ye kind to one another, tender-hearted, for-giving one another."

Now, how interesting this was! Henry and Martin had each got this conqueror's jewel, the grace of God, and it was helping them to get the victory over their selfishness, by teaching them to pray. When the Apostle Paul was on earth, he said, "I can do *all things* through Christ strengthening me." And you and I may say the same.

Edward Norton was a good, obedient boy. He was industrious in his studies, kind to his play-fellows, and usually gentle in his manners; but he had one great fault—a very quick, fiery temper. He would fly into a passion in a moment, and when he was angry he did not seem to know or care what he did. This made his mother very uneasy. She sometimes trembled when she thought of what might happen some day if her dear boy did not learn to control his temper, and get the victory over himself. She told him about the professor in a medical college in Boston, who got angry with a gentleman he was talking with, struck him a blow, and killed him on the spot. He was put in prison; tried, condemned, and hung as a murderer. And she used to say that if that gentleman's mother had only taught him to control his temper when a boy, he never would have become a murderer.

Edward was very fond of reading about the great generals and conquerors of the world. His mother tried to teach him that the greatest and best of all heroes was the one who conquered himself. And in order to fix this lesson on his mind, she made him repeat every morning for a week the thirty-second verse of the sixteenth chapter of Proverbs, where Solomon says, "He that ruleth his spirit is better than he that taketh a city." And every day as she did this, she taught him to pray that God would help him to control his temper, and give him the victory over himself.

On Saturday at the close of this week, Edward was playing with some of his companions. Presently a difficulty arose. He said something about it, when one of the boys began to laugh at him. Edward grew very red in the face. His eyes were flashing with anger; he was doubling up his fist, and just going to strike the boy, when—suddenly he stopped. His hand was unclinched. His half-raised arm fell by his side. The boys did not know what it meant. But the thing that stopped him was the thought of Solomon's words, which he had been repeating all that week. As he remembered them, he offered a silent prayer,— "Lord help me." He tried to keep down his arm, and not speak the angry words. God heard his prayer, and helped him. He gained a splendid victory over himself. His fiery temper met with a Waterloo defeat that day. Edward could not play any more then. He made an excuse for leaving the boys. He ran home to his mother. As he entered the house, he said, "I did it, mother; I did it. God helped me, and I did it;" and he burst into tears.

Here we see how Edward Norton had this conqueror's jewel, and how it gave him the victory over himself. The first thing that this conquering jewel, the grace of God, will do for us in our fight against selfishness is, that *it will lead us to pray against it.*

The second thing that this conqueror's jewel will lead us to do in getting the victory over selfishness is—TO STRUGGLE AGAINST IT.

We must not think that praying is to take the place of striving. God only helps those who try to help themselves. Suppose that you and I have to climb up a high mountain. We kneel down at the foot of the mountain, and pray God to help us to get up to the top of it. And then suppose

we should sit down and wait for God to send an
angel to take us in his arms and carry us up
to the top of the mountain. Have we any right
to expect that God would help us in this way ?
Not at all. We might wait all our lives, but we
never should get any help. If we want to get
up the mountain, we must *begin* to climb, and we
must *keep on* climbing till we get to the top, and
while we are doing this God will help us. No
soldier ever expects to gain the victory over his
enemies without a hard struggle.

We have all read about the great victory which
the Duke of Wellington obtained over the Emperor
Napoleon at the battle of Waterloo. But he had
to fight hard all day before he gained that victory.
And so, if we want to get the victory over our
selfishness, we must struggle hard against it.

Let me tell you about a boy named Archie
Taylor, who struggled against his selfishness, and
conquered it by giving way to his brother.

One day after school Archie came bounding into
the house, crying, " Hurrah ! hurrah ! our school is
going to have an excursion next Thursday. Hurrah!
hurrah ! "

" I'm glad of it, Archie," said his little sister
Amy, clapping her fat hands, and entering into
her brother's joy.

"So am I," said Mrs. Taylor, his mother. "I am glad your teacher is so kind to his scholars. But *how* and *where* are you going, my dear?"

"We are going in two big waggons, mother, to River Point. We are to catch fish, and have a splendid feast of good things afterwards. Won't it be nice? Oh, I'm so glad! But where's the milk-pail? It's time to milk old Spotty."

Then he took the bright tin milk-pail, and went off merry as a cricket, whistling a lively tune.

"Oh, I'm so glad for Archie!" said little Amy to her mother as soon as he was gone.

"Yes, it will be very pleasant for him," said Mrs. Taylor; "for what with milking Spotty, taking care of the pigs, doing up other things, and going to school, he don't get much time for play. I'm very glad his teacher is going to give the school this treat."

Just then a stout boy, four years older than Archie, and covered with flakes like snow, came into the cottage wearing a very bright look.

"Only think, mother," said he, "our fellows are going on an excursion next Thursday. Mr. Jones, our employer, has chartered a little steamboat to take all hands down the river to Bam's Island, where we are to have a glorious feast. Isn't that jolly?"

"It is very kind indeed in Mr. Jones," said Mrs. Taylor, "but I'm afraid you can't go, my son."

"Can't go!" exclaimed George, with great surprise; "pray, why not?"

"Be calm, George, and listen," said his mother. "Did you say the excursion was to be on Thursday?"

"Yes, ma'am; but what of that?"

"Well, Archie is going to River Point that day, and you know that both of you can't be from home on the same day, because my arm is too lame to do the house-work."

"Then let Archie stay at home,—I won't," said George in an angry tone.

"What's that you say?" asked Archie, who came in just then with his pail full of milk.

George told his story. Archie looked blank, and said,—

"I'm the youngest, and I told mother first. You ought to let me go, George."

"Well, I work hard in the mill all the time. You don't earn any money, and you ought to let *me* go," said George.

The boys would probably have got into a quarrel about it, but just then their mother called them to tea, and told them not to say anything more about it till the morning.

They sat round the table and took their tea in silence that night, and with less pleasure than was usual in that humble cottage.

When supper was over, they had prayers as usual. And when Mrs. Taylor came to pray for her children, she asked God to teach them to seek each other's happiness rather than their own; she prayed that He would help them to struggle against the selfishness of their own hearts, and to get the victory over it.

This prayer of their mother's set both the boys to thinking. It was hard for either to give up, yet each felt it to be his duty to do so. Archie was the first to yield. It cost him a mighty struggle; but the next day, when George came home from work, he went to him, smiling in the greatest good humour, and said,—

"George, you may go on Thursday; I'll stay at home."

"No, no, Archie," said George; "you may go, and I'll stay at home.

And now the two brothers had a very pleasant dispute about this. They both wanted to do right, and each with great good nature, pleaded to be allowed to stay at home. At last they agreed to leave it to their mother to decide which of them should go. She said,—

"George shall go, because he works hard for us all the year. Archie will stay at home with me." This was certainly a wise decision. It settled the question at once.

On Thursday morning, George went down the river in the steamboat. Archie stayed with his mother and Amy. As he was getting a pail of water for his mother, his schoolmates rode by in the waggons. He felt pretty badly when he heard their merry shouts come ringing across the meadow. His heart was so full that he did not dare to stop to look after them. But, like an April cloud, this feeling of sadness soon passed away, and he felt happy again. His mother cooked a chicken for dinner; after that, she took Archie and Amy, and they had a walk along the brook which ran past their cottage, and a nice long ramble through the woods. The day soon passed. George came home at the close of the day in excellent spirits; but when they all went to bed at night, the happiest heart in that humble cottage was Archie's, for he had struggled against his selfishness, and had gotten the victory over it, by giving up his own pleasure for his brother's.

The next day, when the teacher found out the reason why Archie stayed at home, he was very much pleased. He spoke of it before the whole

school, and praised him greatly. He said Archie
had set them a beautiful example, which he hoped
they would all follow; that he had proved himself a real hero, and had gained a splendid victory
over himself. Archie had this conqueror's jewel,
—the true agate of the grace of God,—and we see
how it made him conqueror over selfishness.

*The third thing that this conqueror's jewel will
lead us to do in getting the victory over selfishness, is*—TO REMEMBER THE EXAMPLE OF JESUS.

Jesus came down from heaven to do *three* things
for us. The first was, to fulfil God's law for us.
The second was, to die for our sins. The third
was, to show us how to live. The Bible tells us
that " He left us an *example* that we should *follow
His steps."*

You know, when we are learning to write, our
teacher sets us a copy. Then we take the word
or sentence that has been written for us, letter by
letter, and try to make others like them. And
just in the same way the life of Jesus is set
before us as our copy. We are to keep it before
us, and try to make our own lives like His.
Being a Christian, means being like Jesus. Now
it is said of Jesus that "*He pleased not Himself."*
Would it not have been much pleasanter for Him
to have stayed in heaven, where all was holy and

good, where everybody loved and honoured Him,
and where the angels sang His praises, than to
have come down to this dark, sinful world to live
as a poor man, to suffer and to die upon the cross ?
Certainly. Would Jesus ever have consented to be
our Saviour, if He had been trying to please
Himself ? Never. He had the most perfect speci-
men of this conqueror's jewel that ever was, and
it gave Him a glorious victory. He was the most
perfect conqueror of self. "He pleased not Himself." Now, let me show how remembering the
example of Jesus helped a little girl to get the
victory over her selfishness.

The name of this girl was Jeannette. She lived
in Germany. One day she went to see a grand
review of troops in the town in which she lived.
She found a very nice place, where she could stand
and see the soldiers as they marched by. She
stood there and waited for them. Just after the
soldiers began to march past that place, Jeannette
saw a poor old woman behind her, trying very
hard to get a peep at the soldiers. She pitied
her very much and said to herself,—

" I should like to see the soldiers march, but it
isn't kind in me to stay in this nice seat, and let
that old woman stand where she can't see anything.
Jesus pleased not Himself. If I want to be like

Him, I mustn't give way to selfishness. Then, too, I ought to honour old age, and I will."

So Jeannette called the old woman, and, placing her in her nice seat, fell back herself among the crowd. There she had to stand on tiptoe, and dodge about, aud peep, to catch a glimpse of the splendid procession that was marching by, when she might have seen it all easily if she had only kept her place. Some of the people near said she was a silly girl, and laughed at her. But she did not care for that. She felt that she had done right. And so she had. She was trying to be like Jesus. She remembered His example, and it helped her to get the victory over her selfishness; and this made her feel happier than if she had kept her seat, and seen all the soldiers marching. But this was not the end of it.

A few minutes after, a man, all covered with lace, elbowed his way through the crowd, and, laying his hand on her shoulder, said,—

"Little girl, will you please come to her ladyship?"

Jeannette followed the man to the platform, inside of the crowd. A lady came up to her there, and said,—

"My dear child, I saw you give your seat to that poor old woman. You did right. You acted nobly. God will bless you, my child, for what you have done. I hope you will always try and act in this way. Now, sit down here by me, where you can see everything."

This little girl had the conqueror's jewel,—the Bible agate,—and it helped her to get the victory over her selfishness, by *remembering the example of Jesus*.

I have only one more story to tell you, and that is about a boy who had this jewel, and was helped by it in the same way. His name was Roger Seymour.

He came home from school one day, and flinging down his hat, he said, "It's no use trying any longer, mother: I must give up, and go to fighting, as all the other boys do."

His mother looked at him sadly for a moment, and said, "My dear boy, try a little longer for my sake."

"Mother, I've tried, and tried, until the boys all hoot at me, and call me a coward. I don't care so much for that either; but they say, even the best boys in the school, that they can't respect a boy who won't fight; and I'm sure I don't want to lose the respect of my schoolmates. Mother, you don't know the boys in this town: it really seems necessary to fight now and then, or they'll think you have no spirit."

"I can't bear to think of my son engaging in a street fight, even to gain the respect of his companions," said his mother.

"And I can't bear to think that none of the boys respect me," said Roger, as he went out of the room.

Mrs. Seymour felt very sorry that Roger should have so much trouble in school. But yet she could never think of advising him to put himself on a level with the brutes, by fighting like a bulldog or a bear. She knew that Roger was right in refusing to fight. She felt sure that if he only kept on in this way, by and by the very boys who were now the most forward in urging him to fight, would come to have the greatest respect for him, for this very reason,—that he would not fight. So she resolved to try and encourage him all she could by talking to him about Jesus, and getting him to try and keep His blessed example before him all the time.

Before Roger went to bed that night, she had a nice long talk with him. She told him how Jesus was treated when on earth ; she reminded him of the names He was called,—a glutton, a wine-drinker, a Samaritan (that was considered the name of greatest reproach then), and even a devil ! And yet *He* never fought. He never struck any one a blow. He never spoke a cross or angry word to anybody. " When He was reviled, He reviled not again." " Like a lamb before her shearers, He opened not His mouth."

" Remember, Roger," said she, " that Jesus was once a boy, and He knows just how boys feel. As He was the best man that ever lived, so He was the best boy. And the boys who lived in Palestine when Jesus was on earth, were quite as bad as the boys who live here now. No doubt they did everything they could to provoke Jesus, and make Him angry. But He never quarrelled with them. He never fought one of them. His example is the best and noblest for us to imitate. And we must try to be like Him, if we wish to be good, and great, and happy."

" Oh, mother!" said Roger, " when you talk to me, I feel sure that you are right, and it seems as if it would be easy for me to do as you wish; but when I am with the boys, they talk so differently, that they make me think you are too particular. How shall I keep from being influenced by them, mother?"

" You must pray, you must strive, and you must think of Jesus. This is the only way to get the victory in such cases," said his mother.

After this Roger felt more resolved than ever to keep on the right way.

And it was very well he did feel so, for just after that the boys renewed their attacks upon him with more force than ever. They seemed determined to make him fight. But he was equally determined that he would not do it.

One day, just before school, they had been trying very hard to get up a quarrel with him. But he refused.

" Coward ! coward !" was the cry all round: "he's afraid to fight!"

"Afraid! yes, I *am* afraid to do what I *know* is wrong; and you can't make me do it," said Roger calmly, as he turned from them and went into school.

Oh, what hard work this was! for though he knew it was right, it made him sad to feel that the boys all thought him a mean and cowardly fellow. And this is just one of the hardest things we have to bear in this life.

He had been carrying on this great battle with none but God on his side, for all the boys were arrayed against him; but remember, one with God on his side is in the majority. His teacher had been watching carefully the trial that he was passing through. He was delighted to see the stand that Roger had taken. He admired the true courage, the real heroism, which he showed. He was glad that he had one brave boy in his school, who had manliness and courage enough about him to refuse to fight. And now he thought it was time for him to step in to Roger's help. This teacher was accustomed to talk very freely to the boys about anything that happened. So the first time that Roger was absent from school, he took occasion to say to them,—

"Boys, do any of you know Roger Seymour ?"

"Yes, sir, I do," said one.

"So do I," said another.

"And so do I," said a third.

"We *all* know Roger, sir," said a fourth boy.

"Do you ?" asked the teacher. "I thought you would say that, and yet I don't think that any of you really know him at all; for I have often heard you call him a coward, and say that he wouldn't fight, when the fact is, if *you* knew him as well as I do, you would know that he was fighting every day, and that he really did more fighting than any of you."

"Why, we never saw him fighting," said several of the boys. "Pray, sir, who does he fight with ?"

"With *himself*."

"Fight with himself ! how can he do that?" asked the boys.

"In this way," said the teacher. "You have

often provoked him: he forgave you, because he is trying to follow the example of the meek and gentle Jesus. Then you taunted him and called him 'coward.' He knew that he was not a coward, and he longed to show you that he was not one. He felt that by one blow of his strong right arm he could have put a stop to your persecution of him; but he would not displease his mother, he would not do what she had taught him was wrong. And so he has gone on, day after day, struggling against his own feelings. The battle has been a hard one, but he has come off conqueror. I feel proud of such a scholar. I tell you, boys, Roger Seymour is a real hero. He is the bravest boy in the whole school, for *he has conquered himself.* And the Bible says, 'He that ruleth his own spirit is better than he that taketh a city.'"

After that day Roger had no more trouble in school. No one called him a coward again; but they all respected and honoured him more than any boy in the school.

Now Roger Seymour had this conqueror's jewel, —the true agate,—the grace of God, and you see how it made him conqueror. Selfishness was the enemy over which this jewel gave him the victory. And we have spoken of three things that this conqueror's jewel—the grace of God—will help us to do in fighting against selfishness. The first is, *to pray against* it; the second is, *to struggle against* it; and the third is, *to remember the example of Jesus.*

I hope my dear young friends, you will all try to get this precious jewel. You never can fight against the sin of selfishness unless you have it. And you must either fight against it and conquer it, or give yourselves up to it and be its slaves. Now, to be the slave of selfishness is a terrible thing. Jesus came into the world as the Captain of our salvation, on purpose to save us from this sad state. Oh, pray earnestly to Him to give you His grace, and to put this conqueror's jewel round your neck; then you will be able to struggle against selfishness and conquer it. This is the most splendid and important of all victories. May God help you all to gain it, for Jesus' sake. Amen.

The Wonderful Eyes.

" The eyes of the Lord are in every place."—PROVERBS xv. 3.

WHEN we are very much pressed with engagements, it would sometimes be a great convenience if we could manage to be in two places at the same time. But we know that this is impossible. However much we may try, *this* is something that we cannot do. And it is not only true that *we* cannot do it, but it is equally true that the best and wisest and greatest persons in the world cannot do it.

Suppose that a convention should be held in London next year to consider this subject, and this convention was to be composed of five hundred of the best and wisest men that have lived from the beginning of the world. Suppose that Abraham, and Moses, and Job, and Solomon, and Elijah, and Isaiah, and Daniel, and Peter, and John, and Paul, were to be members of that convention; and Christopher Columbus, and Martin Luther, and George Washington, and Benjamin Franklin, and Sir Isaac Newton, and Sir Humphrey Davy, and others of the same

118

character were to be there, what a wonderful convention that would be!

How interesting it would be to see those great and good men, and hear them talk! And suppose that, with all the wisdom and knowledge they had when they were in this world, and with all the higher wisdom gained since they left this world, they should spend a week or a month in trying to find out some way in which a person might be in New York, or Boston, or London, at the same time, they never would succeed. However much a man may know, and however wise and good and great he may be, still he only can be present in one place at a time. This is as true of angels as it is of men. The angels can go very quickly from one place to another; but still, even the angels can only be in one place at a time. We may learn to travel much faster than we can do now. How much faster a locomotive travels than a snail! Now, it is possible that we may learn, by and by, to travel as much quicker than the fastest locomotive goes now, as that exceeds the snail's slowness. Perhaps we may learn to go as fast as a cannon-ball goes when shot from a gun. We may even learn to go as fast as light travels. This is two hundred thousand miles in a second. Only think of this! At that rate we could go to California, and back again, more than ten times in a single tick of a watch or snap of a finger. But even if we could travel at that rate, we could only be in one place at a time. But the Bible tells us that what is impossible with men is possible with God. He can be not in *two* places only at the same time, but in twenty, or in five hundred. Nay, " the eyes of the Lord are in *every* place."

But suppose some one should say this only means that God keeps moving about from one place, without being in every place at the same time, how can we prove that this is not so ? There is one short and easy way of proving this. Here it is : God knows all that everybody thinks, and feels, and says, and does ; and therefore, He must be always present with everybody. *This* is one of the most wonderful things about God. And it is one of the things in which there is the greatest difference between ourselves and God. We can only be in *one* place at a time ; but " the eyes of the Lord are in every place."

Our present purpose is to speak about " The Wonderful Eyes." There are three things that these eyes are intended to do, and on account of which they may well be called wonderful.

The first thing for which " the eyes of the Lord are in every place," is for—WARNING.

You know when there are dangerous rocks at the entrance of a harbour, it is usual to build a lighthouse near them. The lighthouse is put there on purpose to give warning to the sailors of the danger to which they are exposed from those rocks.

There is safety in the light thus given. It used to be the custom with shopkeepers to have strong shutters to their shop windows. When night came they would close those shutters and fasten them very tight with iron bolts or bars. This was done to keep the robbers out. But now it is getting to be the custom not to have shutters at all to the shops. The windows are left with perhaps only a grating of wire before them. But the gas is kept lighted in the shop. If robbers should get into the shop at night, the watchman, or anyone else going by, could see them in a moment. The light in those shops is a better protection than the strongest shutters that could be made. Do you suppose that any person would be willing to go into a shop and steal, if he knew that some one was looking at him all the time? No. And so, if people would only remember that "the eyes of the Lord are in every place," it would be like leaving the window open and the gas burning. It would be a warning against sin. Joseph remembered this; and when he was tempted

to do something very wrong, he said, " How can I
do this great wickedness, and sin against God ? "
The thought of God's eye being upon him was a
warning to him.   And so it will be to us.   Do
you think men would ever allow themselves to
lie, or swear, or steal, or commit murder, if they
could hear the voice of God speaking to them, or
see the eye of God looking at them all the time ?
No.   This is what David meant when he said,
" I have set the Lord always before me : He is
at my right hand, therefore shall I not fall."   To
fall here means to sin, or to do anything wrong.
He felt that, so long as he remembered that God
was near him, and looking at him, it would be a
warning or safeguard to keep him from committing sin.   It is only because we forget what the
Bible tells us about God seeing us, or because we
do not believe it, that we fall into sin.

Let me tell you of a dreadful case of wickedness, which might have been prevented if the
words of the text had only been remembered.

There were three girls in the same class in a
boarding-school.   Their names were Jane, and Lucy,
and Mary.   Jane was the best scholar of the three.
She kept at the head of her class all the time.
Lucy was not as smart as Jane ; but she was very
amiable and loving, and she and Jane were bosom

friends. Mary was neither as bright a girl as
Jane, nor as good a girl as Lucy. She was ill-
tempered and jealous. It used to make her angry
that she could neither recite her lessons as well
as Jane, nor be as much of a favourite as Lucy
was. She envied Jane her success in keeping at
the head of her class, and Lucy her amiability,
which made everybody love her so. She let this
wicked feeling stay in her heart. It grew worse
and worse. From envy it turned to hatred. This
feeling grew stronger and stronger in her bosom,
till it seemed to take entire possession of it. At
last she made up her mind to have revenge on
her classmates in a most awfully wicked way.

At different times she got small quantities of
poison, till she thought she had enough to kill
one, or both, of her classmates; then she waited
for an opportunity to give it to them.

This came rather sooner than she expected.
Jane, the one whom she hated most, was taken
sick with a cold. Her friend Lucy waited on
her, and nursed her like a sister. One evening
Mary was in the room with them. Lucy was pre-
paring a cooling drink of lemonade for her sick
friend. While she was busy in another part of
the room, Mary contrived, without being seen, to
slip the poison into the tumbler. Soon after,

without knowing what had taken place, the kind-
hearted girl Lucy took up the tumbler and carried
it to Jane to drink.   But, happily for her, she
had just fallen into a sound sleep.   In the mean-
time, Mary had left the room.   She supposed, of
course, that the lemonade had been taken; but it
was left on the table untasted.   Soon after, a
servant came in; and, as Jane was still asleep, the
tumbler of lemonade was carried out with some
other things, and left on the table in the dining-
room.   Supposing that the poisoned drink was
doing its deadly work, this wicked girl, in going
up to her own room, passed through the dining-
room.   Seeing a glass of lemonade on the table,
and feeling thirsty, she picked it up and drank
it.   How awful the punishment which overtook
her!   *It was the same tumbler which she had intended should be the means of killing one of her
class-mates, whom she hated most, and of fixing
the blame of the dreadful deed on the other.*
The deadly draught which she had designed for
another, God in His mysterious providence had
caused her to drink herself!

She was soon taken with terrible sickness.   Her
awful screams rang through the house.   The family
gathered round her bed, and were filled with horror
when they heard, from the wicked girl's own lips,

the dreadful deed she had done; and how God had caused her to fall into the very snare which she had laid for another. She died in fearful agony.

Now suppose that, when the thought of this horrible wickedness first came into the mind of this unhappy girl, she had remembered the words of our text,—"The eyes of the Lord are in every place;" suppose she had felt that God was looking right into her heart, and that He was angry with her for her wickedness,—do you think she would have gone on to do what she did? No. The thought of those wonderful eyes would have been a warning to her. It would have kept her from committing that great sin.

Some hundreds of years ago, in what are called "the Middle Ages," the great lords and knights of the world were always at war with each other. In those days there was a celebrated duke, who lived in a great castle. One of this man's neighbours had offended him, and he resolved to take vengeance on him. It happened, soon after he had made up his mind to do this, that he heard his enemy was about to pass near his castle with only a few men with him. It was a good opportunity to take his revenge, and he was determined not to let it pass.

He had a minister of the gospel living in the castle, who was his chaplain. He told him what he was going to do. The chaplain tried to persuade him to give it up, but in vain. He said a great deal to the duke about the sin of what he was about to do, but still he was resolved to go on. Finding that all his arguments had no effect on the duke, the chaplain said to him,—

" Well, my lord, since I cannot persuade you to give up this plan of yours, will you at least come into the chapel that we may pray together before you go ? "

The duke consented, and the chaplain and he knelt down together in prayer. Then the minister said to him, " Will you please repeat after me, sentence by sentence, the prayer which our blessed Saviour taught his disciples ? "

" I will," said the duke.

And so they began, and went on. The chaplain said a sentence, and the duke repeated it, till they came to the petition, " Forgive us our trespasses, as we forgive those who trespass against us." Here the duke stopped.

" My lord, you are silent," said the chaplain. " Please go on, and repeat the words after me— ' Forgive us our trespasses, as we forgive those who trespass against us.' "

" I can't do it," said the duke.

" Well, then, God cannot forgive you, for He has

said so. He Himself has given us this prayer. Therefore you must either give up your revenge, or give up saying this prayer; for to ask God to pardon you as you are pardoning your enemy, is to ask Him to take vengeance on you for all your sins. Go now, my lord, and meet your enemy. In the same way God will meet you at the last day."

This was more than the duke could stand. His stubborn will gave way under it.

"No," said he, "I will finish my prayer: My God, My Father, pardon me; forgive me, as I desire to forgive him who has offended me; lead me not into temptation, but deliver me from evil!"

"Amen," said the chaplain.

"Amen," repeated the duke, who now understood the Lord's prayer better than he had ever done before, because he had begun to practise it.

Now the only way to make men feel that God is present with them, and looking at them, is by causing them to understand His word. God can see us in other ways, but we can only see Him clearly and properly through the truths of the Bible. And so you see that when that chaplain was trying to make the duke understand the meaning of that part of the Lord's prayer, he was really trying to bring him to a point where he would see and feel that the eyes of God were

on him; that he was watching all the feelings of
his heart, and was writing them down in His
book, to judge him for them at last. And as
soon as he saw that "the eyes of the Lord" were
upon him in this way, it was a solemn warning
to him, which he could not neglect. It made him
give up at once his sinful feelings of revenge. If
that wicked school-girl could have been made to
feel that God's eyes were upon her, it would have
kept her from the great sin she had committed,
and have saved her life. And so we see how the
revengeful duke was led to give up his sin as soon
as he felt that God's eyes were on him. "The
eyes of the Lord are in every place." The first
thing for which they are there is for *warning.*

*The second thing for which these wonderful eyes
are present, is for*—ENCOURAGEMENT.

When Moses was leading the children of Israel
through the wilderness, from Egypt to the land of
Canaan, he had a great many heavy trials to bear,
and a great many hard duties to perform. He
needed a great deal of encouragement in bearing
those trials and doing those duties. And the way
in which he got that encouragement was by remembering that God was with him, and His wonderful eyes were watching him all the time. This
is what St. Paul means when, in speaking about

the trials of Moses in the wilderness, he said that "he endured as *seeing Him who is invisible.*" He remembered that these wonderful eyes, which are in every place, were with him even there. He went about all the time, feeling, and saying to himself, "Thou God seest me." And this gave *him* encouragement, and it will do the same to us. If we learn to see "Him who is invisible," that is, if we always remember that "the eyes of the Lord" are upon us, night and day, wherever we go, it will give us encouragement both to *suffer* and to *do* what God appoints to us.

There is a story told of the MacGregors, a Highland clan in Scotland, which illustrates this part of our sermon very well. There was a severe battle fought between the English and the Scotch, at a place called Prestonpans, in the year 1745. In the course of this battle the chieftain of the MacGregor clan was struck by two balls, at the same moment, and fell to the ground. This disheartened his soldiers very much. They thought their beloved chieftain was dead; and having no one to lead them, their ranks began to waver, and they were just on the point of turning their backs on the enemy, and retreating from the field of battle, when their wounded chief raised himself on his elbow, and, as the blood streamed from his wounds, cried out, "I am not dead, my children; I am looking at you. Do your duty like brave men." Those few words had a wonderful effect on the men. All thought of retreating was given up. They were inspired with fresh courage. They felt that the eyes of their chief were upon them, and they plunged into the thickest of the fight, resolved to do honour to the name they bore.

And if we remember that, wherever we go, "the eyes of the Lord" are upon us, and He is watching us all the time, it will be a great encouragement to us. If we have trials to bear, there is nothing that will encourage us like the thought that God's wonderful eyes are watching us.

A gentleman was talking with a poor woman in his neighbourhood, whose case was very trying. She had not been very long married before her husband was taken very ill. He got better after a while, but the disease had fastened itself upon him. He was liable to be attacked by it every few days. This made him unfit to do much work, and even when he did work a little he suffered dreadfully. This was a great trial. Here was a young woman just starting in her married life, when a dark cloud seemed to settle down on her. She was disappointed in all the comfort and happiness she had looked forward to when she was

married. Now she had nothing to expect but
sickness and suffering to her husband, and a long
struggle with poverty and want for herself and
family. She was a Christian woman, as her
answer showed when the gentleman asked her if
she did not feel very unhappy, as she thought of
the trial that was before her. "Well, sir," she
said, "I dare say I should; but when I saw the
trouble coming I made up my mind never to forget these two things: God sees it all, and He
knows what is best. And *when I think that His
eyes are upon me, I feel encouraged to bear up.*"

Yes, "the eyes of the Lord are in every place,"
on purpose to encourage His people.

*The third thing for which these wonderful eyes
" are in every place," is*—TO HELP.

A lady, in one of our large cities, had been in
the habit of attending the evening meetings of the
church to which she belonged. Sometimes she had
no one to go with her, and then she never hesitated to go alone, rather than stay away. Some
of her friends used to tell her that it was a
dangerous thing, and they tried to persnade her
that she had better give it up; but she always
said that the Lord was present in the street as well
as in the church, and she felt sure that He would
take care of her. One evening, in coming home

from church, as she was crossing a public walk
that lay in her way, and where it was quite
lonely, two ruffians stopped her, and, holding a
pistol to her breast, demanded her watch and her
money. But although alone, as they supposed,
there was One with her in whom she trusted,
though they could not see him. It was the same
Saviour at whose presence, when He was on earth,
a whole band of men once "went backward and
fell to the earth." As there was no one but Jesus
to protect her, this Christian lady instantly fell
on her knees before the robbers, and, with up-
lifted hands, cried out, "Now, Lord Jesus, help
me!" This was something for which the robbers
were not prepared. They were frightened, and ran
away, leaving her, all untouched, to go home in
peace, rejoicing in that God whose "eyes are in
every place," and who is a very present help in
time of trouble.

One of the principal ways in which God helps
His people to do right, is by causing them to
understand His word, and feel its power; and
when some verse of Scripture is explained to us,
and set before us in such a way as to make a
deep impression on our minds, then it is just as
if God's wonderful eyes were fixed upon us, to
lead us to do something which He wants to have

done, and to help us to do it. Let me give you an illustration of this.

Julia Morrison was a Sunday-school girl, about thirteen or fourteen years old. She was a Christian girl, and took the greatest delight in her Sunday school, because she loved the Bible so much, and found such great pleasure in studying it there. One day their lesson in school had been on that passage of Scripture in which these words were found: "Whatsoever thy hand findeth to do, do it with thy might; for there is no work, nor device, nor knowledge, nor wisdom in the grave, whither thou goest." The teacher said a great deal about the importance of doing *at once* whatever we have to do. She said, when any duty was before us which we ought to do, we should feel as if the eyes of the Lord were upon us, and He was watching to see if we did it. The teacher's words made a deep impression on Julia's mind. She kept thinking about them all the way home. She said to herself, "I'll always try to remember the lesson of to-day. I'll think I see God's eyes looking straight at me when I have anything to do, and I'm sure it will keep me from putting off things. It will help me to do what ought to be done right away; and it will help me to do it well too, or, as the Bible says, 'with my might.'"

When Julia reached home, she found her father sitting in an easy-chair by the fire, doing nothing. Mr. Morrison was a member of the Church, but he was not a very active Christian. He had undertaken to be a tract distributor in a district of the town, not far from where he lived. He generally took a Sunday afternoon, once a month, to distribute his tracts; but he did not like the work much, and was glad of any excuse for putting it off. It so happened that *that* afternoon was the time for doing this good work. But it had rained a little, and was rather damp, so he had concluded not to go on that day.

When Julia came in, she saw the bundle of tracts lying on the table, and said,—

" Why, pa, haven't you been round with your tracts to-day ? "

" No, my dear."

" Aren't you going with them, pa ? "

" Not to-day, my dear. It's too damp."

Then Julia's lesson came into her mind, and she thought this was a good opportunity to begin to practise it. She had often been with her father when he distributed the tracts. She knew all the places where they were left, and she liked to do it very much, for she felt it was doing something for Jesus. It seemed to her that it was *her* work

as much as her father's. When she saw the bundle
of tracts on the table, she felt as if the eyes of
the Lord were upon her, watching to see what
she would do. That thought helped her very
much. So she said,—

"Oh, pa, let me go with you! I've got my
bonnet on, and it won't take me long."

"No, no! It's too damp for you to go out
again. It'll do as well some other day."

"See, it's not raining now, pa. I'll take the
big umbrella, in case it should rain again. The
people will want the tracts. Do, please, let me
go, pa."

Seeing how earnest she was about it, he said she
might go. So Julia took the tracts, and started.
She knew the district well, and felt very happy
to think that she was working for Jesus. In the
course of her walk she came to a large old house,
with a big knocker on the door. She rapped again
and again, but no one answered. The poor girl's
patience was almost worn out, when she thought
she heard a sound in the house. She gave another
knock, and the door was opened by a middle-aged
woman, who wore a good dress, but whose face,
Julia thought, looked very unhappy.

With a sweet, pleasant smile she handed her a
tract, and then went on her way till her work

was done. When her tracts were all given away,
she went home; but in doing so how little she
thought that, by her walk that damp afternoon,
she had been the means of saving a soul from
death, and a body from the grave.

And yet, it was even so. For it was afterwards
found out that the woman at whose door Julia
had waited so long was in a great deal of trouble.
She had got to be so gloomy and unhappy, that
she did not want to live any longer. She had
made up her mind to hang herself, and was in the
very act of doing this, when this dear girl gave
the first knock at her door. The rope was fastened
to the high post of an old-fashioned bedstead; the
noose, or slip-knot, was round her neck, and she
was going to jump off the bedstead, and rush into
the presence of God, when that knock came at the
door. This startled her. She waited a moment.
There was another knock. She waited longer.
Again and again the knock came. She felt vexed
and angry; but she concluded to go and see what
it was all about. She took the rope from off her
neck, and went to the door to see who had disturbed her. She opened the door. The sweet,
loving, happy look which that dear child gave her,
took away all her angry feelings in a moment.
She received the tract, and concluded to sit down

and read it through, before going upstairs again to carry out her wicked purpose. She did so. God blessed the reading of that tract to her soul's good. It showed her what a sinner she was. It led her to Jesus. She became a Christian; and then she went to Julia's father, and told him what a blessing his daughter's visit to her house had been.

Here you see that it was the thought of God's wonderful eyes being upon her, which helped this dear child to "do with her might what her hand found to do" that afternoon; and how much good came from what she did!

"The eyes of the Lord are in every place." These eyes are wonderful for three things. They are wonderful *to warn;* wonderful *to encourage;* and wonderful *to help.*

My dear young friends, if you will only take the words of this text, and keep them before you all the time; if you will only think about these wonderful eyes, and remember that you never, for one moment, can get away from them,—it will be a blessing to you all your days. It will be a warning,—an encouragement,—a help.

I will finish this subject with some simple lines, which would do us all good if we would learn them, and remember them. They were written on

the words of our text: "The eyes of the Lord are
in every place."

"God can see me every day,
When I work and when I play ,
When I read and when I talk,
When I run and when I walk ,
When I eat and when I drink,
When I sit and only think ;
When I laugh and when I cry,—
God is ever watching nigh.

When I'm quiet, when I'm rude,
When I'm naughty, when I'm good ;
When I'm happy, when I'm sad,
When I'm sorry, when I'm glad ;
When I pluck the fragrant rose,
That in my neat garden grows ;
When I crush the tiny fly,—
God is watching from the sky.

When the sun gives heat and light,
When the stars are twinkling bright ;
When the moon shines on my bed,—
God still watches o'er my head,
Kindly guiding lest I stray,
Pointing to the happy way :
Night or day, at church or fair,
God is near me everywhere ! "

Acknowledging God.

"In all thy ways acknowledge Him."—Proverbs iii. 6.

AMONG the studies that we have to attend to when going to school are spelling and definitions.

We all know something about these studies. We have had many a lesson of this kind. Well, suppose we try our hand at it again. We may begin our sermon to-day with an exercise in the old line of spelling and definition. There is a word of three syllables which we may spell and define, as a sort of introduction to our sermon. The word to which I refer is not a hard one. It is the word—*atheist.*

If I should ask one of you to spell it for me, you would stand up and say—a t h e—athe—i s t, atheist.

And then, suppose I should turn to some one who was further advanced, to some one who has a little college learning, and understands about Latin and Greek, and ask him for a *definition* of the word atheist. He would tell me, in a minute, that this word is made up of two Greek

139

words—viz., the Greek letter alpha, or *a*, which means no; and the Greek word *theos*, which means God. So that the real definition of this word is —no God. And if you want to know what kind of a person an *atheist* is, according to the definition of this word he is a *no-God man*. He is a man who *has* no God; who says or thinks there is no God.

The Bible tells us that such a man is a fool. The Psalmist says, " The *fool* hath said in his heart—no God."

Sir Isaac Newton was one of the most learned men that ever lived. He was an astronomer, that is, he studied all about the stars and other heavenly bodies. He was also a good Christian man. But there was another learned man, and astronomer, who used to visit him sometimes, whose name was Halley. This man was an atheist, a no-God man. He told Sir Isaac one day that he did not believe any one ever made the great worlds which they studied about. He thought they just happened to come where they were.

Sir Isaac wanted to show him the folly of thinking so. In order to do this, he had two globes made,—one to represent the earth, and the other to represent the sky. They were finished in the most beautiful manner. When they were done, he had them placed on the table in the midst of his study, and then invited his friend Halley to come and see him. As soon as he entered the study, his eye rested on the globes. He hastened up to them, and asked, in admiration, " Why, Newton, who made these ? "

" Nobody made them," said Sir Isaac.

" Pooh ! pooh ! " cried Halley ; " then how in the world did they get here ? "

" They just happened here," said he.

" Oh, nonsense, man ! somebody must have made them, for how could they get here of themselves ? "

Then Sir Isaac began and reasoned seriously with him about his own folly, in refusing to believe that those poor little globes could exist without a maker, or come there of themselves, while the great globe on which he lived, and the other worlds around it, he thought had no Maker, but just came by chance.

There are very few people in the world who are willing to profess themselves atheists, or to deny with their *lips* that there is a God ; but there are a great many people who deny God in their lives. They live as if there were no God. They are *practical* atheists. Solomon's words, in the text, are intended to keep us from being like them. Our text says to each of us, " In all thy ways acknowledge Him," that is, God. To acknowledge God, means to own or to confess Him. It means that we should admit that there is a God, and then try to live and act all the time as if we *believed* what we said.

But what is there about God that we should acknowledge? This is the question for us to answer. And in trying to answer this question, I wish to show that there are *three* things connected with God which we should acknowledge.

The first thing about God we should acknowledge is—His PRESENCE.

The Bible teaches us that "the eyes of the Lord are in *every place,* beholding the evil and the good." In the one hundred and thirty-ninth Psalm, David asks the solemn question: "Whither shall I go from Thy Spirit? or whither shall I flee from Thy presence? If I ascend up into heaven, Thou art there: if I make my bed in hell, Thou art there. • If I take the wings of the morning, and dwell in the uttermost parts of the sea; even there shall Thy hand lead me, and Thy right hand shall hold me. If I say, Surely the darkness shall cover me; even the night shall be light about me. Yea, the darkness hideth not from Thee; but the night shineth as the day: the darkness and the light are both alike to Thee." How beautifully

Dr. Watts has expressed this thought in one of his
sweet hymns, when he says :

> " Among the deepest shades of night
>   Can there be one who sees my way ?
> Yes, God is as a shining light
>   That turns the darkness into day.
>
> When every eye around me sleeps,
>   May I not sin without control ?
> No ; for a constant watch He keeps
>   On every thought, of every soul.
>
> If I could find some cave, unknown,
>   Where human feet had never trod,
> Yet *there*, I could not be alone,
>   On every side there would be God."

All people except an atheist—a no-God man—
will admit the truth of this with their lips, and
yet very few admit it in their lives. Yes, very
few people indeed live all the time as if they
believed God was present with them, watching
what they did, listening to what they said, and
reading all their thoughts and feelings and writing
everything down in His great book of remem-
brance. If we only did this, it would soon make
good Christians of us all. In reading the Bible,
you will notice that all the good people of God
whose histories are written there acknowledged
God's presence. They seemed to act and speak
and live, all the time, as if they felt that God

was looking at them. Look at Joseph in the house of Potiphar, in Egypt. He is tempted to do what would have been very wrong. And how does he overcome the temptation ? By acknowledging God's presence. He says, " How *can* I do this great wickedness, and *sin against God ?* " He felt that God was looking at him all the time, and this kept him from committing sin.

Look at Moses. You remember what great trials and troubles he had to pass through in getting the whole nation of the Israelites out from Egypt, and then leading them, for forty years, up and down that waste howling wilderness. Why, when we think of all the immense labours he had to perform, and the heavy burdens and cares that pressed upon him continually, we cannot help wondering how he ever could endure them all. But the Bible explains it very satisfactorily.. It tells us that " he endured *as seeing Him who is invisible.*" This means that he acknowledged God's presence. He felt that God was with him continually. He seemed to see God looking at him, wherever he went, and whatever he was doing. This made his duties easy and his burdens light.

It was just the same with the other good men of whom we read in the Bible. And if we want to be like them, we must acknowledge God's presence

as they did. We must try to get this great
thought fixed on our minds—" *Thou God seest me.*"

Do you think you would ever tell a lie if you
remembered that God's ear was close to your lips
when you were speaking it, and that He would
write it down at once in His book ? No, certainly
not. Or do you think you would ever allow yourself to do anything you knew was wrong, if you
could see the eye of God looking directly at you
while you were doing it ? Of course not. It is
only when we forget God's presence, and become
practical atheists, that we can go on and commit
sin.

A mother once told her little boy to go to a
carpenter's shop and get some chips. " But," said
the boy, " the carpenter isn't there now, and if he
was there, he wouldn't let me have them." " Never
mind that," said his mother, " you can go and
take them, and he won't know anything about it."
" But," said the little boy, " God will know it,
though." This good boy acknowledged God's presence; but his mother acted like an atheist, like
a no-God woman.

There was a very learned man once, whose name
was Linnæus. He was a great botanist, and wrote
a great deal about plants and flowers. He was a
pious man, and had a constant sense of God's

presence. In order to assist him in remembering that God's eye was always on him, he had these words written over his study door: "*Live innocently, God is present.*"

There was a man once, who was in the habit of going to his neighbour's corn-field to steal grain. One day he took his son with him, a little fellow about eight years of age. When they reached the place, the father told him to hold the bag, while he looked round to see if anybody was watching. He peeped through all the rows of corn, and got upon the fence, and looked all round without seeing any one. Then he took the bag from the child, and began to fill it. "O father!" said the boy, "you have forgotten to look one way." He dropped the bag in a fright, and said, "Which way, child?"—supposing some one saw him. "You forgot to look up to the sky, to see if God was watching," said the little boy. The father felt this rebuke of his child so much, that he left the corn in the field, returned to his home, and never ventured to steal again.

There was a little girl whose name was Anna. Her parents were not Christians. They never prayed. When they gathered round the table to their meals, they never asked a blessing, or acknowledged God as the giver of all their mercies.

And when the day was passed, they lay down at night, I will not say like heathen, but like animals, never thanking God for all His favours, or asking Him to take care of them while they slept.

At length there came a pious uncle to spend a few weeks with them. During his stay, he was invited to ask a blessing on their meals, and to conduct family worship.

The morning after he had left them, the family gathered round the table, and were about to commence their breakfast without a word of blessing, when little Anna, who sat next her father, looked up to him, and whispered, " Is there no God to-day, papa ? " This touching question of his child went straight to his heart. It led him to think about his forgetfulness of God, and he soon became a Christian.

A lady was once in a dreadful storm at sea. In speaking of it, she says : " We were for many hours tossed about in sight of dangerous rocks. The steam-engines would work no longer ; the wind raged violently, and all around was heard the terrific roar of the breakers, and the dash of the waves as they broke over the deck.

" While we lay thus at the mercy of the waves, I was comforted and supported by the captain's child, a little girl of eight or ten years old, who was in the cabin with us. Her father came in several times during the lulls of the storm to see his child; and the sight of the captain is always cheering in such a time of danger. As the storm increased, I saw the little girl rising on her elbow and looking eagerly towards the door, as if longing for her father's coming again. He came at last. He was a large, rough, sailor-looking man. He had on an immense coat, great sea-boots, and an oilskin cap, with flaps hanging down his neck, streaming with water. He fell on his knees on the floor beside the low berth of his child, and stretched his arm over her, but did not speak.

"After a while he asked her if she was afraid. 'Father,' said the child, 'let me be with you, and I will not be afraid.

"'With me,' he said; 'why, my child, you could not stand on the deck an instant.'

"'Father, do let me be with you,' she repeated.

"'My darling, you would be more frightened then,' he said, kissing her, while the tears were rolling down his rough weather-beaten cheeks.

"'No, father, I will not be afraid if I am only with you. O father! do let me be with you;' and she threw her arms round his neck, and clung fast to him. The strong man was overcome. He folded her in his arms, and, wrapping his huge

coat about her, carried her with him. The storm
was howling dreadfully, but, quiet as a lamb, that
dear child knew no fear because she was nestling
in her father's arms."

And when the child had left the cabin, the lady
passenger said to herself, " Let me learn a lesson
from this child. She is not afraid in her father's
arms. And have I no father ? Is not God my
heavenly father ? Are not His everlasting arms
round me ? Then why should I be afraid ? " This
thought took away all her fear. She felt that
God was with her, and found sweet peace and
comfort in the thought, till the storm was over,
and the vessel arrived safely at " the haven where
they would be."

In this way we should acknowledge God's *presence*. This is the first point.

But, secondly, we should acknowledge — God's
POWER,—as well as His presence.

We learn from the Bible that God's power is
so great that He can do whatsoever He pleases.
Nothing is impossible, nothing is too hard for the
Lord. And all the power that God has He loves
to make use of—to help His people when they
have hard work to do, to strengthen them when
they have heavy burdens to bear, and to comfort
them when they have sore trials to pass through.

Look at David. When he went to fight the lion and the bear who stole the kid from his flock, he acknowledged God's power by asking Him to help him; and He did so. And then when he came to fight the great giant, whose very appearance frightened the whole army of Israel, he did just the same thing. He told Saul, you remember, when Saul thought he was not strong enough for such a fight, how he fought and killed the lion and the bear. And then he said, " The God who delivered me out of the paw of the lion, and out of the paw of the bear, He will deliver me out of the hand of this Philistine." In this way David acknowledged God's power; and you know how God helped him.

And look at Shadrach, Meshech, and Abednego. Nebuchadnezzar said they must bow down and worship his graven image. They said they would not do it. The king threatened to throw them into the fiery furnace if they did not do it. They said their God was able to keep the fire from hurting them if He chose; but anyhow they would not worship a graven image. Thus they acknowledged God's power; and you all know how God protected and blessed them for it.

And there are a great many instances out of the Bible in which God's people have acknowledged His power, and have been protected and blessed by it.

In a large house that stood in a lonely place in the south of England, there once lived a lady and her two maid-servants. They were a good way off from all other habitations; but they trusted in God, and dwelt in peace and safety. It was the lady's custom to go round the house with her maids every evening to see that all the windows and doors were properly fastened. One night she had been round with them as usual, and seen that all was safe. The servants left her in the entry, close to her room, and then went to their own chamber, which was quite at the other side of the house. As the lady entered the room, she saw distinctly a man hidden away under her bed. What could she do? Her servants were far away. If she screamed, they would not hear her; and even if they came to her help, what could three weak women do against a desperate housebreaker? How, then, did she act? She felt that nothing but the power of God could save her. She lifted up her heart in silent prayer to God for help. Thus she acknowledged His power. She honoured God by trusting Him. We shall see directly how God honoured her.

Quietly she closed the door, and locked it on

the inside, as she was in the habit of doing.
Then she leisurely brushed her hair, and, putting
on her dressing-gown, she took her Bible, and sat
down to read.   She turned to the ninety-first
Psalm, which speaks so beautifully of God's watch-
ful care over His people by night and by day,
and she read it aloud.   Only think how sweet
and comforting it must have been, as she read on,
to feel as if God were speaking these precious
words to her: " He that dwelleth in the secret
place of the Most High shall abide under the
shadow of the Almighty.   He shall cover thee
with His feathers, and under His wings shalt thou
trust.   Thou shalt not be afraid for the terror by
night, nor for the arrow that flieth by day.   Because thou hast made the Lord, even the Most
High, thy habitation ; there shall no evil befall
thee, neither shall any plague come nigh thy
dwelling.   He shall call upon me, and I will
answer him ; I will be with him in trouble ; I
will deliver him and honour him."   When she had
done reading, she knelt down and prayed, still
uttering her words aloud.   She committed herself
and her servants to God's protection.   She told
Him of their helplessness and dependence on Him.
She pleaded the promises she had just been reading in His blessed word, and prayed that she

might find those promises fulfilled in her own experience. Then she put out the light, and lay down in bed; but she did *not* sleep.

A really brave and heroic woman she was. No soldier on the battle-field ever showed truer courage than she did. After a while she heard the robber come out from under the bed. He stood by her bedside. He spoke to her, and told her not to be frightened. Says he, " I came here to rob you; but after the words you have read and the prayers you have offered, nothing on earth would induce me to hurt you, or touch a thing in your house. But you must remain perfectly quiet, and not attempt to interfere with me. I shall now give a signal to my companions which they will understand, and then we will go away, and you may sleep in peace; for I give you my solemn word that no one shall harm you, and not the smallest thing belonging to you shall be disturbed. But, before I go, you must give me the book you read out of; I never heard such words before. I must have that book." She gave him her Bible. He then went to the window and whistled softly. He returned to her bedside, and said, " Now I'm going. Your prayer has been heard, and no evil has befallen you." He left the room, and all was quiet. The lady fell asleep in the sweet

peace with which her trust in God had filled her
heart.

When the morning dawned and she awoke, we
may imagine how she poured out her thanksgiving
and praise to Him who had "defended" her "under
His wings," and "kept" her "safe under His
feathers," so that she was not "afraid of any
terror by night." The robber proved true to his
word, and not a thing in the house had been
taken.

The lady heard nothing more of the robber for
a number of years. One day, however, she was
attending a Bible society meeting in a town in
Yorkshire. After several clergymen had spoken,
a man who was employed as a colporteur of the
society rose to speak. He told this story of the
Lady and the Robber, in order to show the wonderful power of the Bible. He concluded it by
saying, "*I was that robber.*" The lady rose in
the meeting, and said, "It's all true; I am the
lady," and sat down again.

But perhaps some of you may be ready to say,
"Well, I've never been placed in danger like this,
or had such an occasion of acknowledging God's
power." Yes, but then you can acknowledge that
power in little things as well as in great things.

A minister was once trying to show his people

the importance of acknowledging God's power by
praying to Him in trouble. Said he, " I knew a
little boy, about thirty years ago, who had a sore
hand. It became so bad that the doctor thought
it would have to be cut off, to save the boy's life.
On hearing this, the little boy went to a retired
part of the garden, fell on his knees, and prayed
God, for Jesus' sake, to save his poor hand. The
next day, when the doctor came he found the
hand much better ; and a few days after, he said
it would not be necessary to take it off. The boy
lived to be a man ; he became a minister ; " and
then, raising his hand, he said, " This is the hand.
I hold it up before you, as a proof of the benefit
of acknowledging God's power in prayer."

" Do you have any hard lessons to learn ? " said
a gentleman one day to a little school-girl.

" Yes, sir," she replied ; " some of my lessons are
very hard ; but I pray to God to help me to learn
them, and after I have prayed they seem easy."

That is the best way in the world to learn hard
lessons, or to do anything else that is hard.   I
have found out, long ago, that it is the best way
to make the writing of hard sermons easy.

Sometimes wicked people deny the power of
God, and He makes them feel it in a dreadful
way.   There was a company of woodcutters, some

time ago, on the banks of the river Kennebec, in Maine. They were talking one night of the danger to which they were exposed of being killed by the falling timber, as they were cutting trees in the forest. One of them was an infidel. "Nonsense!" said he, "I'm not afraid. God Almighty isn't quick enough to kill me with a falling tree."

The next morning, he went out with his companions to work. The first tree they went to work upon was a fine large one. They have laboured away on it for some time; it is nearly cut through; it begins to lean and crash; they stand aside; it comes thundering down; but before it fairly reaches the ground, a branch lodged on the top of a slender spruce is hurled with fatal aim, as if by the hand of God; it strikes the infidel on the head, and, without a word, he falls to the ground a corpse.

"In all thy ways acknowledge Him." We should acknowledge *God's power.*

And then we should acknowledge—God's PROMISES.

The Bible is full of promises. There are promises here for the young, and promises for the old; promises for the rich, and promises for the poor; promises for the sick, and promises for the well; promises for the living, and promises for the dying. The Apostle Peter calls them "exceed-

ing great and precious promises." They are all
sure promises. When God gives them, He means
just what He says in them. He never has broken
one of these promises. He never will break them.
And when we believe these promises, and live and
act just as if we expected to find them fulfilled,
then we acknowledge God, so far as His promises
are concerned.

Look at Jacob. He went away from his father's
house, you remember, when he was a young man.
The first night he spent on his journey he had an
interesting dream. He saw a ladder, which reached
from earth to heaven, and the angels of God were
going up and down on it. God came to him in
that dream, and said He would never leave him
nor forsake him, but would keep him in all his
journey, and bring him back at last in safety to
his father's house. That was God's promise to
him. Jacob believed it; and years afterwards,
when he was going back to his father's house, he
was in great trouble. His brother Esau was
angry with him, and came against him with an
army of four hundred men to kill him. Jacob
was greatly alarmed. He had no help but in God.
He prayed earnestly to Him. He reminded Him
of the promise given him years before, that He
would bring him home again in safety. He

pleaded with Him to fulfil that promise, and to keep Esau from hurting him. God heard that prayer; He remembered that promise; He caused Esau's feelings to become entirely changed towards Jacob, so that when he came up to him, instead of smiting him with the sword as he had intended to do, he fell on his neck and kissed him, and was just as kind to him as he could be.

And God remembers His promises in just the same way now, and fulfils them, when His people acknowledge His promises, and pray to Him in faith to fulfil them.

Not long ago, during a very dry summer, some of the midland counties of England were suffering greatly for want of rain. Several pious farmers who were afraid of losing their crops unless they should soon have rain, agreed with their minister and others to hold a special meeting at their church, for the purpose of praying for rain. They met accordingly, and the minister, coming early, had an opportunity of talking to some of the people before the meeting began. While he was thus engaged, he was surprised to see one of his little Sunday-school scholars walk into the church, staggering under the weight of a huge old family umbrella.

" Why, Mary, my child," he said " what in the

world made you bring that great umbrella on such a bright beautiful morning as this ? "

The dear child looked up into his face, feeling surprised that a minister should ask such a question, and said, " Why, sir, as we are going to pray to God for rain, and God has promised to hear and answer His people when they pray, I thought I'd be sure to want the umbrella."

The minister felt reproved by the simple faith of this dear lamb. You see how this child acknowledged God in regard to His promises. Well, shortly after, the meeting was opened. While they were praying the wind arose ; the sky, before so clear and bright, became overcast with clouds ; and soon, amidst vivid flashes of lightning and heavy peals of thunder, a storm of rain burst upon the country. Those who came to the meeting without properly acknowledging God's promises, and not expecting to receive the blessing they came to ask for, had to take a soaking on their way home for their want of faith, while Mary and her minister returned together under the large old family umbrella.

Here is an example of a poor widow woman, who was in great distress with her little ones, but who acknowledged God's promises, and obtained from Him the help that she needed.

THE WIDOW'S PRAYER.

In the winter of 1875, in the state of Iowa, in
America, the snow fell early in November to the
depth of two feet.   The storm was so great that
neither man nor beast could move against it.   In
a log cabin, six miles from the nearest house,
lived a widow with four children; the oldest was
eleven years of age, and the youngest a baby, only
a year old.   Her supply of food and fuel was
very small when the snow began falling.   Day
after day the stock melted away, until the fourth
evening.   Then the very last morsel of food was
eaten for supper, and there was not wood enough
left to keep the fire going for another day.

That night, according to her custom, she gathered
her little ones around her, and read to them out
of God's blessed book.   Among the verses that she
read were these words of the Psalmist : " I have
been young, and now am old ; yet have I not seen
the righteous forsaken, nor his seed begging bread."
" The lions do lack and suffer hunger, but they
that wait on the Lord shall want no good thing."
Then she kneeled down with her helpless little
ones, and prayed to God.

She told the Lord that their food was quite
gone, and their fuel almost gone.   She pleaded

the promises from His holy word which had just
been read. She asked God to fulfil those promises in this hour of their great need, and to send
them such help as they required. She believed
that these promises would be fulfilled. Then they
went to bed, and slept soundly.

When the next morning dawned, that mother
arose. She kindled the fire and put the kettle on,
as she was in the habit of doing; although now,
for the first time in her life, she had nothing to
put in it. But she felt sure that something would
come, because she believed that God's promises
never fail.

While she was waiting by the fire, a man in a
sleigh drove up to the house. He knocked at the
door. As soon as she opened it, he came in and
asked if they were in want of anything. Her
heart was so full that it was some time before
she could speak. But soon recovering herself, she
told him how they had eaten their last morsel of
food the night before, and then had called on God
to help them.

He was greatly surprised at what he heard.
Then he said to her, " Last night, about nine
o'clock, my wife and I both had the thought come
into our minds, that there were some one in this
cottage needing help. We could hardly sleep any

during the night for thinking about it. As soon as it was light this morning, I hastened to come out and inquire about it."

Then he went to his sleigh, and brought into the house bread and flour and meat and groceries; and so the grateful mother had an abundant supply from which to prepare for her little ones a substantial breakfast, although they had gone to bed the night before without a particle of food in the house.

And during the day, the same kind-hearted person sent the poor widow a load of wood. And thus all her wants were supplied, by that God whom she had so truly acknowledged, by faith in His promises. And when we know that the person who brought this help was a stranger to the widow and her family, and when we see that the thought of sending this help came into his mind *at the very time when the distressed mother was crying to God for help*, we may be very sure that the thought did not come there by chance, but *that God put it there*, and that it was in this way He answered her prayer for help. She had acknowledged God in His promises, and so He fulfilled those promises by sending to her in that unexpected way, the help that was needed by herself and little ones.

"In all thy ways acknowledge Him."

We have seen that there are three things about God we should acknowledge; these are, His *presence*, His *power*, and His *promises*.

Let us remember these three *p*'s.

When Jesus was on earth, He said to His disciples, "Without Me ye can do nothing." We cannot acknowledge Him properly without His help. Let us pray for His grace to help us, and then, wherever we go, let us acknowledge His presence, or carry the thought of Him with us. Let us acknowledge His power, by praying for His help in all that we have to do. And let us acknowledge His promises, by expecting and praying to have them fulfilled for our relief and comfort, whenever we are in trouble and sorrow.

I was reading lately of a dear little boy, only three years old, who beautifully practised the lesson which the text teaches. His mother had been out nearly all day, and came home at night, feeling very tired and unwell. She went early to bed to get a good night's rest. But the little boy was not tired at all and disposed to talk a great deal. At last his mother said, "Charley, mamma is sick and tired, and can't talk to-night."

"Ma," said he, "God can make you well, can't He? Shall I ask Him?"

" Yes, my dear," said his mother.

Charley hopped up in bed, and kneeled down on the bed-clothes, and folding his little hands together offered this prayer: " O good heavenly Father, please to make my dear mamma well by morning for Jesus' sake." Then he crept back into bed, and in a few minutes he was asleep. When he awoke in the morning, his first question was, " Are you well this morning, mamma ? " Without thinking of what had taken place the night before, his mother said, " Yes, my dear, I am very well this morning." " Oh, I knew you would be," said Charley, clapping his hands for joy ; "I knew you would be, for I prayed to God to make you well, and *Jesus always hears little children when they pray.*"

That is the kind of trust in God we ought all to have. Then, "in all our ways we shall acknowledge Him." I will close my sermon with some sweet lines about trust in God :

> " Happy, Saviour, should I be,
>   If I could but trust in Thee ;
>   Trust Thy wisdom me to guide,
>   Trust Thy goodness to provide ;
>   Trust Thy saving health and power,
>   Trust Thee every day and hour ;
>   Trust Thee as the only light,
>   In the darkest hour of night ;
>   Trust in sickness, trust in health.

Trust in poverty and wealth ;
Trust in joy, and trust in grief,
Trust Thy promise for relief ;
Trust Thy blood to cleanse my soul,
Trust Thy grace to make me whole ;
Trust Thee living, dying too,
Trust Thee all my journey through ;
Trust Thee till my feet shall be
Planted on the crystal sea ;
Trust Thee, ever-blessèd Lamb !
Till I wear the victor's palm ;
Trust Thee till my soul shall be
Wholly swallowed up in Thee !"

The Cure for Care.

'And Abraham called the name of the place Jehovah-Jireh."—
GENESIS xxii. 14.

THE place here spoken of, was that to which
Abraham went to offer up his son Isaac as a
burnt-offering. Abraham was living, when this
took place, at Beersheba, in the southern part of
the land of Palestine. God came to him one
night, and told him to take his only son Isaac,
whom he loved, and offer him for a burnt-offering,
on one of the mountains in the land of Moriah,
which He would show him. This was a very
hard thing for a loving father to do with his
only son. But Abraham never hesitated. He
"rose up early in the morning," and went to do
what God had told him. After travelling three
days, they came to the place. It was Mount
Moriah to which God led him. This was the hill
around which the city of Jerusalem was afterwards built. Solomon made a level place round
this hill, and then built his temple over the top
of it. People who visit Jerusalem now can go
and see this interesting spot. We had this pleasure

during our stay in the Holy City. The mosque
of Omar stands where Solomon's temple once stood.
The beautiful rounded dome of that mosque—called
the "Dome of the Rock"—rises directly over a great
mass of rock, which is the top of Mount Moriah.
I looked at that huge rock with great interest.
As I stood gazing at it, I said to myself, "There,
on top of that rock, is the very place to which
Abraham came with his son Isaac. There he
built an altar, and laid the wood in order upon
it. There he bound Isaac, and laid him on the
wood. There he took the knife to slay his son,
and there, as he was holding that knife to his
son's throat, God called to him from heaven. He
told him not to slay his son, and showed him a ram
caught by his horns in a thicket, which he was
to offer as a sacrifice instead of his son."

What a relief to Abraham that must have been!
Yes, and what a relief to Isaac too! How glad
he must have felt, when his father took him down
from the altar, and unbound his limbs! What
thankfulness must have filled his heart, as he felt
himself snatched from a sudden and painful death!
I thought I could see the happy boy, wiping the
big drops of sweat from his brow, and looking
around on everything about him, as one would do
who had never expected to see them again.

After such an experience as this, we do not wonder to find it said, "And Abraham called the name of the place Jehovah-Jireh." Jehovah means *Lord.* It is the most sacred name for God the Bible tells us of. The word " Jireh " means *will see,* or *will provide.* And so Jehovah-Jireh means "the Lord will provide." One reason why all this was allowed to happen to Abraham on Mount Moriah, was to teach him how easily God can provide for His people, whatever is necessary for their help and comfort. And God has caused this interesting story to be written in the Bible, on purpose that we may learn the same lesson too. If we learn the lesson well that is taught by these words, Jehovah-Jireh, " the Lord will provide," it will be of great use to us. In going through this world, we all have a great many cares and troubles to meet. These are like heavy burdens that we have to bear. It is a great blessing to know what is the best way of getting rid of these burdens, or if we cannot get rid of them, to find out how to bear them with the greatest ease and comfort. Nothing will help us to do this better than the words of our text, if we learn clearly to understand, and firmly to believe, the lesson they teach.

This lesson is *the cure for care,* which the Bible

furnishes. We are taught this lesson by the words
which Abraham used when he said, "Jehovah-
Jireh—the Lord will provide."

It will help us to learn this lesson, and to get
rid of our care, if we remember three things that
God provides for His people.

*The first thing that God provides for His people
is*—PROTECTION IN DANGER.

It is wonderful how many illustrations we find,
both *in* the Bible and *out* of it, of the way in
which God provides protection in danger for His
people. When we open the Bible for these illustrations, they meet us everywhere. There is the
great ark, in which Noah and his family were
protected from the deluge of water which drowned
the world. Look at it, as it goes floating securely
over the face of the troubled waters ; and it seems
as though we could see " Jehovah-Jireh, the Lord
will provide," written in large letters all over it.
And when we turn from this, and think of the
tiny ark of bulrushes which floated on the quiet
waters of the river Nile, and protected the infant
Moses from the cruelty of Pharaoh, we see another
illustration of the same truth. And when we
remember how Joseph was protected from the
wicked intentions of his brethren ; and how the
whole nation of the Israelites were protected from

the dangers of the wilderness, during the forty
years of their wanderings there; and how David
was protected for ten years, while Saul was trying in every way to kill him; and how Jonah
was protected when thrown into the sea; how
Daniel was protected from the hungry lions, and
his three friends from the fierce flames of the
devouring furnace,—we see how full the Bible is
of illustrations of our text, "Jehovah-Jireh—the
Lord will provide."

But there are plenty of illustrations of this
truth to be found outside of the Bible. The
animal and the vegetable kingdom afford us plenty
of illustrations of this same truth. Look at the
scales of the crocodile, and the thick, tough hide
of the rhinoceros, and the powerful trunk of the
elephant, and the strength and courage of the lion.
Look at the turtle, with the castle that it carries
with it, and the snail crawling along with its
house on its back. When you see how God
provides for the protection of all these different
creatures, you see how each of them illustrates
the truth which Abraham was taught on Mount
Moriah, when he called the name of it Jehovah-
Jireh.

A friend of mine has a very powerful micro-
scope. One day he showed me some curious

specimens through it. Among these were some
tiny little sea animals. They were so small that
they could not be seen with the naked eye. They
are made to live on the rocks under the water;
and, to protect themselves from being swept away
by the force of the waves, they are furnished
with the tiniest little limbs you ever saw. Each
of these is made exactly in the shape of an
anchor. This they fasten in the rock; and as I
looked at them with wonder through the micro-
scope, I thought: Why, even among these very
little creatures we see Jehovah-Jireh too! The
Lord provides for *their* protection.

And every apple and pear and peach and plum
that grows shows the same thing, in the skin
which is drawn over them for their protection.
And so does every nut, in the hard shell which
grows round its kernel. And so does every grain
of wheat, and every ear of Indian corn, in the
coverings so nicely wrapped around them to keep
them from harm.

And God is doing wonderful things all the time
for the protection of His people.

A Christian sailor, when asked why he remained
so calm in a fearful storm, said, " If I fall into
the sea, I shall only drop into the hollow of my
Father's hand, for He holds all these waters there."

A lady was once riding in her carriage over a mountain road. She saw a beautiful flower springing up by the side of a great rock. She got down from her carriage, and thought she would take up the little flower and plant it in her greenhouse. But, small and delicate as that flower was, she found it impossible to remove it, because its roots ran under the great rock by whose side it grew. And as she took her seat in her carriage again, she thought to herself, " Just so Jesus, the Rock of ages, shelters those who trust in Him." And that little rock-protected flower seemed, as it grew in its beauty, to be saying to all who went by—" Jehovah-Jireh."

Little Bessie was in bed. Nurse came in, and found her lying wide awake.

" All alone in the dark ! " said nurse, " and not afraid at all, are you, Bessie, darling ? "

" No, indeed," said Bessie, " for I'm not all alone. God is here. I look out of the window, and see the stars ; and God seems to be looking down on me with all His eyes."

" To be sure," said nurse, " but God is up in the sky, a great way off."

" No," said Bessie, " God is here too, and sometimes He seems to be *clasping me in His arms;* and then I feel so happy ! "

That little child might go to sleep saying, "Jehovah-Jireh, the Lord will provide" for my protection.

A young widow, with two children, was living in the city of Berlin. She was a Christian woman, and trusted in Jehovah-Jireh to take care of her. One evening she had to be away from home for a while. During her absence a man entered her house, for the purpose of robbing her. But "the Lord who provides" protected her from this danger in a very singular way. On returning to her room, she found a note lying on her table, which read as follows :—

"MADAM,—I came here with the intention of robbing you ; but the sight of this little room, with the religious pictures hanging round it, and those two sweet-looking children, quietly sleeping in their little bed, have touched my heart. I cannot take anything of yours. The small amount of money lying on your desk I leave untouched, and I take the liberty of adding ten pounds besides."

The Bible tells us that "the hearts of men are in the hands of God, and He turneth them as the rivers of water are turned." He turned the heart of this robber from his wicked purpose, and in this way He protected the widow who trusted in Him.

One morning a Christian farmer, in Rhode Island, put two bushels of rye in his waggon, and started to the mill to get it ground. On his way to the mill he had to drive over a bridge that had no railings to the sides of it. When he reached the middle of this bridge, his horse, a quiet, gentle creature, began all at once to back. In spite of all the farmer could do, he kept on backing, till the hinder wheels went over the side of the bridge, and the bag of grain was tipped out, and fell into the stream. Then the horse stood still.

Some men came to help the farmer. The waggon was lifted back, and the bag of grain fished up from the water. Of course it could not be taken to the mill in that state. So the farmer had to take it home and dry it. He had prayed that morning that God would protect and bless him through the day, and he wondered what this accident had happened for. He found out, however, before long.

On spreading out the grain to dry, he noticed a great many small pieces of glass mixed up with it. If this had been ground up with the grain into flour, it would have caused the death of himself and his family. But Jehovah-Jireh was on that bridge. He made the horse back and throw the grain into the water, to save that family from the danger that threatened them.

Protection in danger is one thing that God will provide for His people. The recollection of this should help to cure care, or to keep us from being too anxious.

" Jehovah-Jireh—the Lord will provide."

*The second thing that God provides for His people is—*RELIEF IN TROUBLE.

There are many troubles that we meet with as we go on through life, and in which no one can give us such relief as God can. Sometimes people are in trouble, because they want to get information in regard to something on which their comfort depends, and God is the only one who can provide relief for them, by giving them the information which they need.

Here is a striking illustration of the way in which God can provide this relief, when it is needed. Some years ago there was a Christian man in England, who was in trouble. He was poor, and suffered much for want of money. A valuable property had been left to him. It would be sufficient to make him comfortable all the rest of his life, if he could only get possession of it. But in order to do this, it was necessary to find out some deeds connected with this property. But neither he, nor any of his friends, could tell where those deeds were to be found. They had tried to find them for a long time; but all their efforts had been in vain. At last, God provided relief for this man in his trouble in a very singular way.

On one occasion, Bishop Chase, who was then the Bishop of the Protestant Episcopal Church, Ohio, in America, was on a visit to the city of Philadelphia. He was stopping at the house of Mr. Paul Beck. One day, while staying there, he received a letter from one of the Bishops of the Church of England. This letter was written to Bishop Chase, to ask him to make some inquiries about the deeds relating to the property of which we have spoken. The letter had been sent out first to Ohio, and then to Washington, where the Bishop had been. From there it had been sent on after him to Philadelphia. If Bishop Chase had received this letter in Ohio, or in Washington, he would probably have read it, and then have said to himself, " I can't find out anything about these deeds," and would have written to his friend, the English Bishop, telling him so. But the letter came to him while he was at Mr. Beck's house. Mr. Beck was present when the letter was received. The Bishop read it to him. When Mr. Beck heard the letter read, he was very much astonished. " Bishop Chase," said he, " it is very singular that this letter should have come to you while you are at my house. Sir, I am the only man in the world that can give you the information asked for in this letter. I have the deeds in my possession. I have had them for more than forty years, and never could tell what to do with them, or where to find the persons to whom they belong." How wonderful it was that this letter, after coming across the ocean, and going from one place to another in this country, should reach the Bishop while he was in the house, and in the presence of the only man in the world who could tell about those lost deeds! And if the poor man to whom the property belonged, when he came into possession of it, knew about the singular way in which those deeds were found, he certainly would have been ready to write upon them, in big round letters, the words, "Jehovah-Jireh—the Lord will provide." God provided relief for him in his trouble.

"Mother, I think God always hears when we scrape the bottom of the barrel," said a little boy to his mother one day. His mother was poor. They often used up their last stick of wood and their last bit of bread before they could tell where their next supply was to come from. But they had so often been provided for in unexpected ways, just when they were most in need, that the little boy thought, " *God always heard when they scraped the bottom of the barrel.*" This was only that little fellow's way of saying what Abraham said when he called the name of the place where God delivered him Jehovah-Jireh.

Here is an illustration of the way in which God sends relief in trouble. The story is told by the Christian woman to whom it happened, in her own language :—

" About the month of January 1863, I was living in Connecticut alone, with two little boys, one of them four years old, and the other about a year and a half old. My husband was away in the service of his country. When the coldest weather came, I was nearly out of wood. I went down into the village one day to try and get some, but tried in vain. So many men were away in the army, that help was scarce. Very little wood was brought into market, and those living on the main street got all that came; while those who lived outside the village could get none. I tried to buy a quarter of a cord from two or three merchants, but could not get any. One of them told me he could not get what he wanted for his own family. Another said he was not willing to yoke up his team for so small a quantity; but as I had only seven shillings I could not buy any

more, and so I was obliged to go home without
any.

"I went back to my little ones, feeling very sad.
But while I sat there, almost ready to cry, the
words of Abraham came into my mind—"Jehovah-
Jireh—the Lord will provide." Then I went up
to my chamber. There I kneeled down and told
God of my trouble, and asked Him to help me,
and send the relief that we needed. Then I went
to the window and waited, looking down the street,
expecting to see the wood coming. After waiting a
while, without seeing any come, my faith began
to fail. I said to myself, 'The Lord did provide
for Abraham, but He won't provide for me.' Our
last stick of wood was put in the stove. It was
too cold to keep the children in the house without fire. I got their clothes out, and thought I
would take them to the house of a kind neighbour, where I knew they could stay till we got
some wood. But just as I was going out with
the children, in passing by the window, I saw the
top of a great load of wood coming up the road
towards our little house. 'Can that be for us?'
I asked myself. Presently I saw the waggon
turn off the road, and come up towards our door.
Then I was puzzled to know how to pay for it.
Seven shillings, I knew, would only go a little

way towards paying for all that wood. The oxen
came slowly on, dragging the load to our door.
I asked the man if there was not some mistake
about it. 'No, ma'am,' said he, 'there is no mistake.'

" 'I didn't order it, and I can't pay for it,' was
my reply.

" 'Never mind, ma'am,' said he, 'a friend ordered
it, and it is all paid for.'

" Then he unhitched the oxen from the waggon,
and gave them some hay to eat.

" When this was done, he asked for a saw and
axe, and never stopped till the whole load was
cut and split, and piled away in the woodshed.

" This was more than I could stand. My
feelings overcame me, and I sat down and cried
like a child. But these were not bitter tears of
sorrow. They were tears of joy and gladness, of
gratitude and thankfulness. I felt ashamed of
myself for doubting God's word, and I prayed
that I might never do so again. What pleasure
I had in using that wood! Every stick of it as
I took it up, seemed to have a voice with which
to say, 'Jehovah-Jireh.' As Abraham stood on the
top of Mount Moriah he could say, 'The Lord *will*
provide;' but every day as I went into our
woodshed, I could point to that blessed pile of

wood, sent from heaven, and say, 'The Lord *does* provide.'"

A mother one morning gave her two little ones books and toys to amuse them, while she went up-stairs to attend to something. A half-hour passed quietly away, and then one of the little ones went to the foot of the stairs, and in a timid voice called out, " Mamma, are you there ? " " Yes, darling ! " " All right," said the little one, and went on with her play. By and by the question was repeated, " Mamma, are you there ? " " Yes, darling ! " " All right," said the child again, and once more went on with her play. And this is just the way we should feel towards Jesus. He has gone up-stairs, to the right hand of God, to attend to some things for us. He has left us down in the lower room of this world, to be occupied here for a while. But to keep us from being worried by fear or care He speaks to us from His word, as that mother spoke to her little ones. He says to us, " Fear not : I am with thee." " I will never leave thee, nor forsake thee." " Jehovah-Jireh—the Lord will provide." The second thing that the Lord will provide is relief in trouble. And the recollection of this will help to cure care for us.

*But there is a third thing that the Lord will provide, and that is—*SALVATION FOR THE SOUL.

And this should have a great influence in curing care with us. The soul is the most valuable thing we have. Jesus said that if a man should gain the whole world and lose his soul, he would make a foolish bargain. And Jesus knows what the real value of the soul is better than any one else. He made the soul. And when it was lost, He paid the price that was necessary to redeem it. And when we come to understand the value of the soul, we shall never have any peace or comfort till we know that it is safe. The thought of losing the soul will fill us with care and anxiety. This care will become a burden to us, and we never shall find relief from this burden till we hear the voice of Jesus saying, "Come unto me, all ye that labour and are heavy laden, and I will give you rest."

Here is an illustration of a man who was very much burdened with care on account of his soul, and who had this care cured by the salvation which Jesus provides. Many years ago there was a very celebrated preacher, whose name was the Rev. George Whitefield. He went travelling all over England and this country preaching the gospel, and did a great deal of good in this way. One day a brother of Mr. Whitefield's heard him preach. The sermon led him to see what a sinner he was, and he became very sorry on account of his sins. He was burdened with care because he thought his soul could not be saved; and for a long time it seemed as if he could get no relief from this burden. And the reason of it was that he was not willing to believe the word of Jesus. It is only in this way that we can be saved. When we read the promises of Jesus in the Bible, we must believe that He means just what He says. We must trust His word, and then we shall be saved.

Well, one evening this brother of Mr. Whitefield was taking tea with the Countess of Huntingdon. This was an earnest Christian lady, who took a great interest in all good ministers, and the work they did for Jesus. She saw that the poor man was in great trouble of mind, and she tried to comfort him as they took their tea by talking to him about the great mercy of God to poor sinners through Jesus Christ.

" Yes, my lady," said the sorrowful man. " I know what you say is true. The mercy of God is infinite. I am satisfied of this. But, ah! my friend, there is no mercy for me. I am a wretched sinner, a *lost* man."

"I am glad to hear it, Mr. Whitefield," said Lady Huntingdon. "I am glad in my heart that you have found out you are a lost man."

He looked at her with great surprise. "What, my lady!" he exclaimed, "glad did you say? glad at heart that I am a lost man?"

"Why, certainly I am, Mr. Whitefield," said she; "for you know, Jesus Christ came into the world 'to seek and save them that are lost.' And if you feel that you are a lost man, why, you are just one of those that Jesus came to save."

This remark had a great effect on Mr. Whitefield. He put down the cup of tea that he was drinking, and clapped his hands together, saying, "Thank God for that! Thank God for that!" He believed God's promise then. That cured his care. It took away his trouble. It saved his soul. He was taken suddenly ill and died that same night, but he died happy.

Here is another illustration of the way in which Jesus saves people for doing nothing else but simply trusting in Him. It was given by a minister who was settled in the coal region, and had a good deal to do with miners. He was talking one day with a hard-working miner on the subject of religion. The man had never joined the church, but he was so correct in his conduct that the minister felt sure he must be a Christian. He asked the man if he thought he was a Christian, and what reason he had for thinking so. This was the honest miner's answer,—

" Sir," said he, " you know I am no scholar; but I'll tell you the best way I can why I hope I am a Christian.

" It is not what *I* do that I trust in, but what Christ has done for me. You've been down the shaft into the mine, sir. This will help me to tell you what I mean. For a long time I was trying to do what was right—to live as I ought to; and so was trusting to my own works for salvation. But all the while I felt as if I was still down at the bottom of the shaft. All I could do didn't get me out of the pit. Then God showed me that all my righteousness was but filthy rags, as the Bible says. But how was I to get out of the shaft? Why, at last I found that the only way out of the deep mine into which sin had brought us was to do just as I do when I want to get out of the coal-mine. To do this, I have only to get into the bucket when it comes down, and trust to the men at the windlass to draw me out. And so I find it is about my soul. I can't draw myself out of the pit; but I trust in Jesus, and leave it all to Him. I used to try to do what was right and to serve God, because I was afraid of Him and of the judgment; but now I try to serve and please God because I love Him."

This shows us very clearly the way in which God provides salvation for His people.

Here is another illustration of the same truth. A minister was once visiting an old man who was in great distress and trouble about the salvation of his soul. He had just the same difficulty that the miner had, as mentioned in the last story. He thought he must work himself out of the shaft; he was not willing just to put himself in the bucket, and trust to the men at the windlass to get him out.

At last the minister said to him, " Now, suppose I should go to a shop and buy something for you and pay for it, and tell you to go and get it; would it be necessary to take any money with you ? "

" No," said the old man, brightening up; " it would be paid for."

" Need you make any promises to pay at some future time ? " asked the minister.

" No," he replied; " I should have it for nothing."

" Well, it is just so," said the minister, " with the forgiveness of sins and the salvation of the soul. Jesus has paid the full price for us. The groans, the sighs, the tears, the wrath, the pain, the punishment our sins deserved He took upon Himself; He bore it all; He paid the full price for our salvation. He bought it for us with His precious blood, and He offers it to us, as the Bible says, 'without money, and without price.'"

" Yes," said the old man, as his eyes filled with tears; "I see it now, though I never saw it before. It is pardon for nothing; salvation for nothing. Now I understand what the apostle means when he says, 'Eternal life is the *gift* of God, through Jesus Christ our Lord.' Jesus paid for it, and now God gives it to us *all for nothing.*"

There is just one other story I wish to tell, and this shows us how quickly God can save the soul when he pleases to do so. A Christian father and mother had long prayed for their son, that he might become a Christian and be saved. But it seemed as if their prayers were not to be heard. He grew up to be a careless, obstinate, disobedient boy; and at last he ran away from home and became a sailor.

One day, on board the ship, he had mounted up the rigging, and while there lost his hold and fell overboard. A boat was lowered at once to pick him up; but as the vessel was going very fast at the time, it was a good while before the young man could be reached. At last, however, he was brought on board, though he seemed to be in a lifeless state. The surgeon of the ship used all the means he could to restore him, but all seemed to be in vain. His comrades had given up all hope of saving him when he gave some signs of life. Then they renewed their efforts, and after a while the young man opened his eyes, and cried out in tones of joy, "*Jesus Christ has saved me!*"

Then he was silent again; and it was a good while before he could tell what he had felt in his fall, and while he was struggling in the water. After he was quite recovered, he gave this account of himself:—

"While falling from the yard-arm, as soon as I felt my danger, it seemed as if all the sins of my life stood before me, as quick as the lightning's flash. I saw what a dreadful sinner I was. I was afraid of death, and the punishment to follow. Then this text of Scripture came into my mind; I had often heard my father repeat it: '*This is a faithful saying, and worthy of all acceptation, that Jesus Christ came into the world to save sinners.*' I lifted my heart to Him with the earnest cry, 'Lord Jesus, save me!' He heard my cry. My sins are pardoned; I am saved. I thank God for that fall!"

The result showed that he was sincere. From that day onward he lived a new life. He returned to his parents, and became their support and comfort for the rest of their lives.

www.ingramcontent.com/pod-product-compliance
Lightning Source LLC
Chambersburg PA
CBHW062216080426
42734CB00010B/1906